One Hundred Years – It's a Birthday to be Proud of!

City Council 2002 - 2005

Left to right: Robert Hobson, Al Horning, Brian Given, Colin Day, Mayor Walter Gray, André Blanleil, Barrie Clark, Sharon Shepherd, Ron Cannan

When Kelowna was incorporated in May, 1905, our population consisted of 600 people and farming was the economic mainstay of the region. Today more than 100,000 people call Kelowna home and we've become the main marketing and distribution centre of the Okanagan Valley.

Orchards and wineries attract accolades and tourists from around the globe; while our industrial sector competes on a world scale. Best known for forestry and light manufacturing, Kelowna also has a growing high technology sector that includes aerospace development and service.

Kelowna is considered to be one of the most livable cities in Canada. With virtually all the amenities of a major centre, Kelowna is fortunate to retain some of its small-town charm including a strong sense of community and an appreciation of our valued agricultural heritage.

First Nations peoples and the early settlers first recognized the potential of this favoured lakeside location. It's now our responsibility to protect and preserve the achievements of the past century while moving towards a future filled with promise.

Sincerely,

Walter Gray
MAYOR

Celebrating the achievements of our first 100 years – looking forward to the future.

This special Centennial publication is brought to you as part of the Kelowna Museum's on-going efforts to tell the story of our community. In purchasing this volume, you have demonstrated an important personal step in preserving and in-terpreting that history. The funds raised through the sale of this Centennial Magazine will help position the Kelowna Museum for a strong future role in our community.

Thank you for your support.

Wayne Wilson
Executive Director
Kelowna Museum

Jim Grant
President
Kelowna Museum

Contributing Writers

Wayne Wilson is the Executive Director of the Kelowna Museum and has been working in the Heritage/Museum field for more than 25 years. He has also taught in the Department of Geography at Okanagan University College for 10 years in the Regional and Historical Geography of British Columbia and of Canada. He holds a Bachelors Degree and a Master of Arts Degree from the University of British Columbia.

Robert M. "Bob" Hayes is a life-long resident of Kelowna, with Okanagan roots dating back to the early 1870's. A teacher by trade, he spends much of his spare time in researching and writing about the history of the Central Okanagan Valley.

Sharron J. Simpson grew up in Kelowna and left the community for several years to travel and study. She has had an eclectic career and on returning to Kelowna, established Manhattan Beach Publishing. Her first book wa According to Bill: The Life and Times of C.W. (Bill) Knowles, a sold-out collection of short stories about the early days in the Okanagan. She has also written and published Boards, Boxes, and Bins: Stanley M. Simpson and the Okanagan Lumber Industry – a story about the Interior lumber and orchard industries and the over 600 million wooden boxes produced during the early years of the last century. She is currently working on another volume of stories for one of the community's leading companies.

Sharron is also involved in community heritage issues, is a freelance writer, and has designed and taught the writing course: Memories into Memoirs which is offered in conjunc tion with the Kelowna Museum. The group is about to publish Volumes Five and Six of their unique stories.

Colleen Cornock was born and raised in Kelowna. She possesses a keen interest in local history and has served for two years as a Director for Kelowna Branch of the Okanagan Historical Society. Colleen is the fourth genera-tion of her family to be born and raised in Kelowna and is proud to be able to continue her family's efforts to preserv and celebrate Kelowna's rich history.

Keith A. Boehmer has been a volunteer and employee at the Okanagan Military Museum for five years. He is a past member of the BC Dragoons and active member of the BCD Whizzbangs Association, recently producing a virtual pictorial exhibit that is soon to be launched on the Virtual Museum of Canada's website under the title "Always First - A Pictorial History of the British Columbia Dragoons."

Julianna Hayes is an Okanagan Valley-based wine writer, who has been involved in the industry since 1996. In 2000, she became the wine columnist for the Okanagan Newspaper Group and began producing a bi-weekly on-air commentary on wine for CBC Radio's Daybreak program. Hayes also writes for the Victoria Times Colonist and is editor of the Okanagan Wine Country Tour Handbook. She has served as a judge for various wine-related competitions including the 2003 and 2004 Lieutenant Governor's Awards for Excellence in the BC Wine Industry, the British Columbia Wine Label Awards through The Wine Museum, and the Okanagan Icewine Festival.

C. W. 'Bill' Knowles is a life member of the Okanagan Historical Society and has been a champion, like his father before him, of heritage and preservation in Kelowna. Some of his significant contributions are to: the Benvoulin Church, Guisachan House, Headgate Park, Knowles House and the Laurel Building. For several years he wrote numerous columns for The Daily Courier, and the Capital News. At age 90 he wrote his 'Best Seller' "According to Bill, The Times and Tales of C.W. (Bill)Knowles."

KELOWNA PUBLISHERS
(formerly Pioneer Publishers)
PUBLISHER
Diana Knowles
LAYOUT & DESIGN
Lynne Jensen
SALES ASSOCIATES
Laverine Riviere, Anne Reid,
Edie Laveroff, Diana Knowles
PHOTOS
Kelowna Museum Archives
unless otherwise stated.

Kelowna Publishers
607 Hollywood Road N.
Kelowna, BC VIX 7M2
Phone: (250) 491-4704 email: knowles8@telus.net
PRINTED IN CANADA BY WAYSIDE PRESS LTD.

Inside

5	Culture in the Colony
9	S.S. Sicamous
13	Where's the Tomb?
17	Kelown's Own Auntie Mame
20	Kelowna Regatta
22	George Athans
24	Okanagan Wine
30	Kelowna's Renaissance Man
33	Accomodation
42	A Legend in His Own Time
46	Frontier Health - 1908 Style
47	Kelowna Industry
52	Tobacco
54	An Unlikely Success
58	School Days
68	Which Knox Was it Anyway?
72	The Sporting Life
76	Okanagan Oil
77	Riding the Rails to Kelowna
81	Kelowna and the Spanish Flu – 1918
83	Okanagan Lake Floating Bridge
84	The British Columbia Dragoons
87	Fire Protection
93	Completing the Circle
99	Arts and Culture
103	Chinatown
104	One of the Earliest Pioneers
110	Getting to Kelowna by Boat
115	Flying in to Kelowna
118	The Greening of Kelowna

Proud to Power Kelowna.

FortisBC is a proud sponsor of Kelowna's centennial celebrations.

As we remember 100 incredible years, at FortisBC we're even more excited by the role we're playing in Kelowna's future.

Every day at FortisBC, we're working hard for our customers and neighbours and this means going beyond just keeping the lights on. It means supporting community programs like these celebrations, protecting the environment or saving you money through PowerSense.

And so we can all look forward to a happy, safe future, FortisBC is also dedicated to promoting safe work practices for our employees and raising electrical safety awareness with our customers and the public.

So please remember, if you are working or playing around electrical structures, know your limits. Call us at **310-WIRE** for information on electrical safety.

Mary Pratten came to Kelowna and introduced many little girls – and a few little boys – to an art form and a world beyond the confines of their isolated hometown.

Culture in the Colony
MARY PRATTEN - DANCE TEACHER EXTRAORDINAIRE

By Sharron J. Simpson

The Western Canadian frontier wasn't all beer halls and dancing girls – at least not in Kelowna. Many of the new residents to this remote corner of the Empire brought their elite upbringings along with them and in the early years of the last century, *The Kelowna Courier and Okanagan Orchardist* ran advertisements for "Professors of Music" who offered pianoforte, violin, and elocution lessons. These cultured "professors" were also at liberty to provide concerts, songs, recitations, and monologues. For many, it was their only marketable skill.

There is little doubt however, that they made significant contributions to the early cultural life in the Okanagan. Several elaborately costumed Gilbert and Sullivan light operas were mounted by amateur thespians, with *The Mikado* being a particular favourite. Lequime's General Store at the foot of Bernard Avenue or Raymer's Hall a little further along the block, made space available above their ground-floor shops which, when not being used as school rooms, or church halls, were often filled with audiences enjoying enthusiastic theatrical productions.

While all this was going on in Kelowna, Mary Pratten was completing her ballet training at the Royal Academy of Dance in England. In spite of receiving advanced training in London and Paris, Mary found herself trapped in the prevailing myth that only the Russians produced 'real' ballet dancers, and she eventually discovered that her love of dancing couldn't provide her with a living if she stayed in England.

Mary had few options to pursue her career and, at the age of 35, headed for the colonies and began teaching dance in Toronto, in 1912. A few years later she moved to Winnipeg where she also taught before heading further west, eventually arriving in Kelowna in 1937. Mary's brother, Ted, travelled with her and as much as she was an independent soul, he was the reverse and almost totally dependent on her skills to earn them a living, though he did keep track of the 25¢ or 50¢ she charged her students for lessons.

Stephanie Finch

In the midst of the Depression, Mary and Ted found a little house in downtown Kelowna and, undaunted by the realities of little disposable income and high unemployment, Mary, by now 60 years old, rented the Women's Institute Hall on Glen Avenue – the Hall still stands behind the Armoury on what is now Lawrence Avenue – and began to offer dance lessons to the few thousand people who lived in the small community.

Mary was a pioneer and determined not to compromise her standards or be deterred by the vast distance between Kelowna and the best of British culture. She taught the full syllabus of the Royal Academy as well as the Scottish highland fling and sword dance, the sailor's hornpipe, the Italian tarantella, and the Irish jig. Dance slippers, toe shoes for fledgling ballerinas, and many costumes were ordered directly from England. In a testament to the high regard in which the Royal Academy held Mary, an adjudicator travelled from the hallowed dance studios of London every two years to judge her students in the tiny outpost of Kelowna .

Mary began her classes with a "now, all in your places please ladies," and as she stood in front of the assembled group with pointer in hand to prod an unbent knee or a misplaced foot, she intimidated – likely unintentionally – many of her tiny pupils. This teacher was a strict disciplinarian – dance was an art form – and Mary's lessons were serious and not intended as a fun or recreation. More than one little child went home in tears for not having performed up to the unforgiving teacher's expectations.

Mary Pratten and Pupil

Talented and motivated students were rewarded by being placed in the front row of the class, but if they faltered, it was immediate demotion to the back of the room in disgrace. Students who did well on their Royal Academy exams and won various competitions were further rewarded by having their photo hung on the wall of Mary's tiny living room. Everyone aspired to join that elite group and were enticed by Mary's elusive promise of "one day I hope to see your picture on this wall."

Mary Pratten taught the full syllabus of the Royal Academy as well as the Scottish highland fling and sword dance, the sailor's hornpipe, the Italian tarantella, and the Irish jig.

As the community grew, Mary Pratten's dancers picked up where Mary's turn-of-the- century countrymen had left off, as they participated in every musical production, festival, International Regatta, charitable event, and social engagement in the Valley. Her services were in such demand that Mary set up a second dance school in Penticton in 1948 and, at the age of 71, thought little of commuting down the Valley by Greyhound bus to give her lessons.

Mary Pratten received a cable of congratulations and good wishes from the Royal Academy of Dance on her 80th birthday – she must have been one of their most tenacious and enterprising students – and she continued to teach into her late 80s. Her pupils moved on to join several prestigious dance companies including the Royal Winnipeg Ballet, founded in 1939 by Gweneth Lloyd and Betty Farrally who had also come from England and eventually retired to Kelowna to create The Canadian School of Ballet on the foundation of Mary Pratten's dancing classes.

Mary never wavered from her determination to introduce classical dance in all its beautiful variations, to one very small Canadian community. At an age when most people retire, Mary came to Kelowna and introduced many little girls – and a few little boys – to an art form and a world beyond the confines of their isolated hometown – and did so with such discipline and determination that today, networks of dance teachers and dance studios throughout the Okanagan continue to follow in the footsteps of this very tiny, visionary English dancer.

KELOWNA IS THE HOME OF A CANADIAN DANCE LEGACY

1938 Gweneth Lloyd and Betty Farrally emigrate from Leeds, England to Winnipeg, MB to establish a ballet school. The Canadian School of Ballet (CSB) is founded.

1939 From the CSB the Winnipeg Ballet Club is formed which became The Royal Winnipeg Ballet.

1949 Gweneth Lloyd starts the Dance Division of the Banff Centre for the Arts.

1959 Gweneth and Betty move to the Okanagan to establish the CSB in BC.

1963 The CSB and Kelowna Little Theatre present their first pantomine "Cinderella". This begins a long association with Paddy Malcolm English, playwright and director.

1987 Mel Brown and Lori Larson assume the directorship of the CSB from Lloyd and Farrally.

2002 A dream of the CSB is united with a vision of David LaHay. The formation of Ballet Kelowna, a professional ballet company begins.

The Canadian School of Ballet

BALLET KELOWNA

101-2303 Leckie Rd. Kelowna

7

S.S. Sicamous being Towed
To Rest at Penticton
Aug. 27/51   Kelowna BC.

Ribelin Photo

S.S. Sicamous
SERVICE FROM 1914 TO 1951

By C.W. (Bill) Knowles

As near as I know, I am the only person alive who witnessed the launching of the S.S. *Sicamous* at OK landing in 1914. When my mother read in the paper that the Sicamous was to be launched she put me aboard the first stern wheeler, the S.S. *Aberdeen*, named after Lord Aberdeen who owned large tracks of land near Kelowna and Vernon. She was launched sideways and everything was fine, except she got stuck in the mud; they had forgotten to check the depth of the water. They tied a long, heavy rope to the S.S. *Sicamous* and our boat and I can still remember when the S.S. *Aberdeen* started up. As the rope tightened and the water was flying out of the rope, I was so scared that I made a dive to get under my mother's long white skirt for protection. That didn't pull the boat out so the next day they tied a tugboat and a stern wheeler to her and that got her out.

About a week after we saw the S.S. *Sicamous* being launched we were having breakfast and we heard the heavy roar of the steam horn as she rounded Manhattan Point. We dropped our cutlery and ran down Bernard Ave. to watch her make her first entrance into Kelowna. On a sadder note, I was sitting on the railing of the wharf when she berthed with a few hundred soldiers on their way to the Vernon Army Camp. It was the beginning of World War I and it was the first time I ever saw men crying. I was six years old.

I have many, many memories of riding the S.S. *Sicamous* up and down Okanagan Lake. I remember, on a dark winter night, a crewman walking along the narrow deck on the S.S. *Sicamous* towards a night light, a black box about the size of a small apple box . He would turn a little crank until two points of the arc touched and that would light up the corner of Bernard Avenue and Abbott Street as bright as a hot summer day and that would guide her in.

There was jealousy between Kelowna and Penticton seniors for the tourist trade, but sure none between the teenagers as Penticton was endowed with more then their share of pretty girls. We guys would find any excuse to jump on the S.S. *Sicamous* on weekends to date them. I asked one of the girls if I could take her to the New Year's dance at the Incola Hotel, *THE* hotel in the South Okanagan. After I took her home, I boarded the *Sicamous* again and it looked as if half of Kelowna was on board carrying on the party.

I think you will find this interesting as life was so different then. Roads were practically non-existent, just rough trails so the lake was the only way to get from Penticton to Vernon. Kelowna was much smaller as we were not on a railway and they were. Perhaps I should add that there was one road between Summerland and Penticton and it was so bad that if you dared take it, it took you all day in a horse and buggy.

Actually, boat travel started long before the *Sicamous* or even the *Aberdeen*. Thomas Shorts would row people from Okanagan Landing and later progressed to a small steam engine boat. He would hire people to cut trees along the way, cut them to length to fit the fire box and stack them to dry. To finish Thomas Shorts story, when the S. S. *Aberdeen* was put into service in 1893, Shorts predicted he'd have it out of business in 6 months. It didn't work out that way.

One interesting little story was a young girl who came out from England to Okanagan Landing. She got into the row boat with Thomas Shorts to go to Summerland or Peachland and it shocked her mother when she said they slept on the beach at nights.

The S.S. *Sicamous* had its own 32 volt steam generator and on dark winter nights she was a lovely sight going down the lake past our house at Manhattan Beach with lights by the hundreds along the decks and portals. Another sight we enjoyed was when the lake froze over and the *Sicamous*, with its steel hull (the other boats all had wooden hulls), would

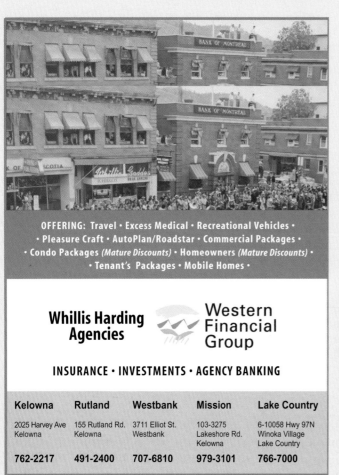
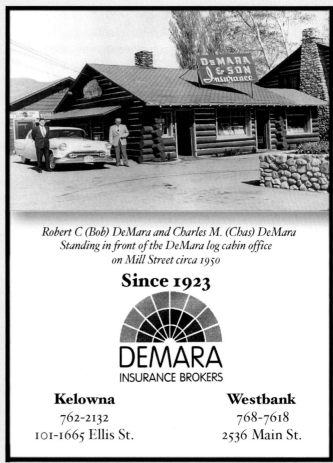

smash the ice and when that failed, a tugboat would push a barge on top of the ice and crush it. It was great entertainment on a cold winter night - no radio or television, just a gramophone. Now Penticton was a different story. From Summerland to Penticton the lake gradually got shallower and of course the ice was thicker. I was fortunate to get a few pictures for my book of when the *Sicamous* failed to break the ice and they brought in the barge and when that didn't work, they used dynamite. I have been very lucky to have lived in the era of the country warming up.

As more people settled in the Valley, they didn't all have wharves so the *Sicamous*, with its steel hull would run up onto the sand or rocky beach and the crew would pass on articles, papers, and food to the residents who signalled the boat by raising a flag.

Over the years, as business declined due to the automobiles taking over and roads being built, the *Sicamous* lost its passengers and the CPR removed one deck and she became a lowly tugboat for 4 years. Then she was put to pasture and anchored at Okanagan Landing only to be vandalised - first the steering wheel and so on down the line. Finally, the CPR offered her to Kelowna who turned her down due to lack of lakeshore and Penticton grabbed her for one dollar as they had no end of lakeshore and have done a first class job of restoration.

Now, my experiences on the tugboats are not as exciting as on the *Sicamous*. Nonetheless, they do cover an experience that few people have had. I can't vouch that it was the *Naramata* I was on, as the lake was crawling with steam tugboats in the summer and fall.

I'll go back to when four of us fellows were about 18 and we canoed to Penticton and down the old winding river to Dog Lake, Skaha Lake today. We had been away a week by now. Paddling up the river was a different story than paddling down. It took four hours going up and only two hours to come down and we were beat. When we spotted the tugboat, Russell Williams and I asked the skipper if we could put our canoes on the bow of the barge, in front of six to eight emptied fruit cars being returned to Kelowna. He said that Russ and I could but Gordon Meikle and Frank Fumerton would have to take the *Sicamous*. We loaded the canoes in front of the cars, put our blankets in the canoes and crawled in. When the tugboat went up the dead-calm lake we had the sensation I am sure no one but tugboat crews ever witnessed. The steam tugboat that pushed the barge was almost silent so Russell and I couldn't hear any engine noise, just the little lapping of water as the barge pushed the water ahead of us. It was eerie.

When we got to Kelowna around 2:00 a.m., we pulled our canoes off quickly so as not to impede the crewmen unloading the empty cars to take to the different packing houses. As the ground was so soft they couldn't run the locomotives over it so Jack Jennens designed and Dave Chapman built a heavy *shunter* truck. Until the CNR rail came to Kelowna in the mid-1920s Bert Marshall, who we went through high school with, spent most of his life operating it.

Going back to Russell and me. It was interesting as we watched how the crew handled the very long steel cable by pulling it perhaps a hundred yards out, pulling it around a huge pulley and back to the cars and fastening it to the first car. Then they started the steam winch and

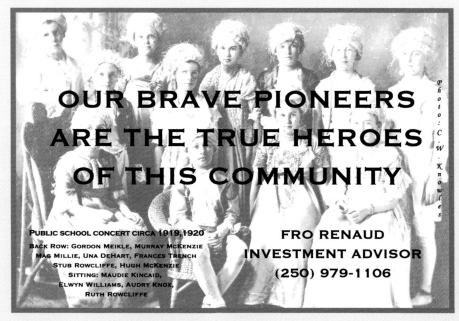

we could hear the wheels screeching all over town as the fruit cars came down off the barge. Many nights, at the same time, I could hear the screeching and knew that the tugboats were in.

Another incident was when, on a quiet Saturday night, I would canoe from our house on Manhattan Beach to the Aquatic Hall dance. I would canoe my girlfriend home (she lived on Mill Creek). Paddling home I would pass the tugboat arriving. All I could hear was the ringing of the bells that the Captain used to give orders to the crewmen. Life was quiet in those days.

It was a far different era than today and I am certainly happy that I lived through it. That age would never have started if the Okanagan Valley didn't have the best climate in Canada. Even through the Depression it kept growing. Dad knew it in 1905 when he arrived here and Kelowna had a population of 500 the year of its incorporation.

When Gordon Meikle and I were teenagers, we spent many weekends camping at Manhattan Beach. We would watch for the *Sicamous* leaving Okanagan Landing. They would pour the coal to the boilers and the black smoke would come out of the smoke stacks and we would know when to paddle our canoes out to the middle of the lake. We would paddle up to the big paddle wheel without getting hit by the piston arm. We wanted to get that one big roller and not get dumped.

At 5 a.m. the deckhands would be roused for the dayshift. With a splash of water for the outside and a bowl of porridge for the inside they'd begin hauling coal on at Kelowna; nine tons of it in a day. "First, we shovelled coal down the chute and later we hauled the ashes up until our hands would get raw", recalls Bill Guttridge of Peachland, who worked on Okanagan Lake's old tugs during the 1940s and 50s. "Coal-up, we'd hose the tug down and when the railcars were ready, we'd winch them on board, block them and then load the other barge."

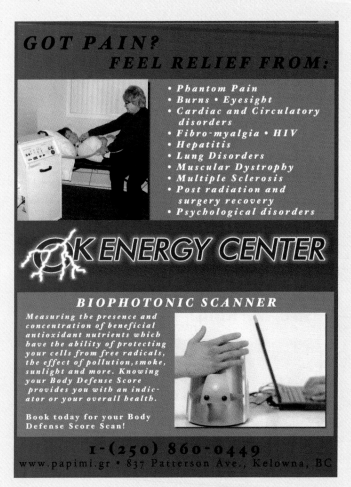

The barge, or two barges, would be tied up alongside the tug for the trip down the lake, unless the weather got rough, then the barges would be towed on a heavy steel cable. Repetition of that scene at different points up and down the lake took up most of the crew's time, with periodic breaks to eat, sleep, and maybe make a little music with such available instruments as spoons, mouth organs and violins.

Guttridge left home in Penticton at sixteen years of age to work for a season as a deckhand on the S.S. *Kelowna*, which transported wooden railway barges with eight railcars, a barge containing fruit, coal, settlers' effects or even hay up and down the valley. Over the fourteen or so years he spent on the Valley's tugs, Guttridge also worked aboard the S.S. *Naramata*, and the M.V. *Okanagan*, a diesel-powered craft, both of which were owned by Canadian Pacific at the time.

As well, Guttridge worked on the Canadian National tugs, No. 6 and the *Pentowna*. I mentioned to Bill that I was probably the only person outside of the tugboat crew to have experienced that eerie sound of water lapping under the bow of the barge on a calm night. He said that he remembered it very well.

Where's the Tomb?
THE REMBLER PAUL STORY

By Sharron J. Simpson

There are several signs around Kelowna's north end pointing out the path to Paul's Tomb. A beautiful trail from Poplar Point winds its way about a 100 feet above Okanagan Lake and surrounds the curious hiker with the full expanse of the Valley's most beautiful views. Another sign points to Paul's Tomb from the first lookout – the Crown Lookout – part way up Knox Mountain, while others are tucked away in neighbouring subdivisions.

All the trails offer hikers opportunities to enjoy the lake, the native bunchgrass, pine forest, and an array of small woodland creatures as well as a uniquely peaceful hour out in the sunshine – or snow, depending on the season.

All paths lead to the same point, but in each case you are left wondering "am I there yet?" And, "if this is called Paul's Tomb, where's the tomb?" Most hikers assume they have arrived because there is a wide spot in the path, a picnic bench, and port-a-potty … but there is no sign pointing to the tomb nor telling its story.

The tomb is there and dates back to 1910 when Rembler Paul, a wealthy unconventional Montrealer, decided to build a family vault on this remote property he had recently purchased, as a permanent and beautiful final resting place for he and his wife.

Rembler and his wife – who only ever seems to have been referred to as Mrs. Paul – also had a substantial property and home on Bernard Avenue, between Bertram and Richter Streets, with stately grounds, shady trees, and glorious

Dignity Memorial® is the largest network of honored funeral, cremation and cemetery providers

Lakeview Cemetery

Conveniently located
adjacent to the Kelowna
International Airport, the
cemetary offers a
beautiful and peaceful
setting overlooking Duck Lake.
Established in the early 1960's it has over
50 years of heritage

Phone 250.765.2929

Valleyview Funeral Home

Valleyview commenced operation
in July of 1976 serving
the Rutland community from its
location at 165 Valleyview Road.
A member of the Dignity Memorial family
of funeral homes, they provide quality service, friendly
and knowledgeable staff, and offer the finest in equipment and

facilities in the Kelowna area.

Phone 250.765.3147

www.valleyviewfuneralhome.com

First Memorial Funeral Services

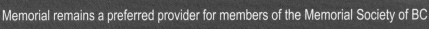

First Memorial was established by the Foreman family in
Vancouver in 1961 with the express
purpose of serving the Memorial
Society of BC.
The Kelowna operation at
1211 Sutherland Avenue
opened in 1983 and is the leader in providing
low cost alternative funeral services. Today, First

**FIRST MEMORIAL
FUNERAL SERVICES**

...the only name you really need.

Memorial remains a preferred provider for members of the Memorial Society of BC

and the general public.

Phone 250.762.2299

www.firstmemorialkelowna.com

gardens. Rembler had been one of the first white men to trap, hunt, and explore for gold on both sides of the Rocky Mountains. He had eventually settled in Regina and bought up large tracts of land which he sold for a substantial profit as the prairie city grew. Rembler had also figured out the benefits of trading wheat futures and made a great deal more money in that venture as well.

Paul was 85 years old when he retired to Kelowna in 1905, an imposing figure of stocky build who was immediately recognizable because of his neatly groomed voluminous white beard. Rembler was generous with his wealth and was known to quietly assist a number of the small town's struggling entrepreneurs. He was also the sole investor in a local gold mine which seemed more rumour than reality, though in 1914 the area was abuzz with the possibilities.

Mrs. Paul fell ill with what was eventually diagnosed as cancer, shortly after the couple arrived in Kelowna, and was bed-ridden for most of her remaining years. The couple's only son had died a few years before and while one of their three grandsons lived with them for awhile, the couple kept a very low profile in the community.

The mystery remains as to why Rembler decided he wanted a tomb, but in 1910 he engaged George Patterson to build the concrete structure. The location of the tomb was inaccessible by road so the cement, wire, reinforcements, and lumber all had to be hauled up the Glenmore Valley by wagon, loaded onto a stone boat and towed up the hill, and then slid down the shale-covered face on the other side.

The tomb was dug into the hillside and its concrete walls and roof were fitted onto a marble base. A seven foot high passageway ran down the middle of the structure with concrete shelves built on either side – enough room for eight coffins. A ten foot high concrete face was attached to the front of the structure and a steel vault door with a combination lock, was then added.

An interesting anecdote remains about the tomb's construction. While Patterson was finishing up the installation and working alone inside, he suddenly realized the vault door had swung shut and he was trapped. Undeterred by the prospect of being entombed alive, he quickly realized that the concrete around the door hadn't completely set so he was able to quickly cut around the door hinges and forced the door outward. He escaped unscathed but likely a bit unnerved by the thought of what could have been.

Mrs. Paul made only one visit to the summer place before her death, travelling overland by horseback and side saddle, as was the custom at the time. Upon her death, the small town's leading citizens turned out for an impressive funeral, and "amid every manifestation of sorrow," followed the coffin from the church to the foot of Bernard Avenue where they boarded a flotilla of boats and followed the coffin to the tomb, five miles north of town. Once they had reached the site, "the patriarchal appearance of the old man, with his flowing white beard, heading the procession up the steep hill from the lake's side, will long live in the memories of those present." The day was sunny, the lake calm, and those presented were deeply touched by the sadness of the occasion.

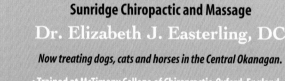

Two years later, in 1916, Rembler himself passed away. He had travelled to Edmonton for the winter and after a slight attach of la grippe, quietly died. His body was returned to Kelowna, by train, and he too was transported up the lake by barge and entombed with his wife. Friends who had accompanied the old man's body to the tomb, stole a quick look at Mrs. Paul's coffin, and noted that she was perfectly preserved inside her copper casket.

Rembler Paul

After Rembler's death, a caretaker moved into the log summer house on the property, though he was unable to prevent vandals from destroying the lock on the steel door, which made it impossible for anyone to gain access to the tomb.

In 1926, the property was sold to Dr. and Mrs. Tucker from Indiana who used it periodically, before selling it to C. W. (Bill) Knowles who, when again unable to stop the vandalism, bulldozed rocks and earth up and over the entrance to the tomb, leaving only a small portion uncovered showing the date the tomb was constructed.

So – yes – there really is a tomb at the end of the trail where two of Kelowna's early residents rest quietly to this day. And yes, it is in the direction the signs are pointing … and if you look carefully, you may be able to see a small crest with the 1910 date still showing. But if you don't discover it – not to worry – the quiet hillside, and easy walk, the beautiful views – and now the story – provide an opportunity to ponder a local curiosity which, in the end, is likely more important than catching a glimpse of the tomb itself.

The Kelowna *Grass Shack* was located at the west end of the newly opened Okanagan Lake Bridge. By the end of the decade, Mernie had expanded and opened *Grass Shacks* in Radium Hot Springs, Kamloops, Nelson, Victoria, Prince George, Calgary, and West Vancouver. With Heather as her on-the-spot model, Mernie showcased Hawaiian bathing suits, cover-ups, strapless summer dresses, and muu muus.

Kelowna's Own 'Auntie Mame'

MERNIE PURVIS

By Sharron J. Simpson

Heather's Sportswear opened in the old Tudor-styled Royal Anne Hotel on Bernard Avenue, in 1948. The elegant shop was a revolutionary alternative to the small town department stores which offered the usual dry goods and little cotton dresses that seemed to be the uniform of every housewife in town.

The shop's owner was Mernie Purvis, a reluctant stay-at-home wife and mother, and since Jim, her husband, travelled most of the time as sales manager for GE appliances, Mernie decided to branch out on her own and see where her fashion flare would take her.

Her first venture was *Heather's*, named after her young daughter, Heather, and Mernie quickly found her niche by offering cashmere sweater sets and kilts as an upscale alternative to the more conservative shops in town. Shopping became fun, the new store was an immediate success, and it wasn't long before she opened a second *Heather's* at the Prince Charles Hotel in Penticton.

Heather's Sportswear **opened in the old Tudor-styled Royal Anne Hotel on Bernard Avenue in 1948. The elegant shop was a revolutionary alternative to the small town department stores which offered the usual dry goods and little cotton house dress that was the uniform of every housewife in town.**

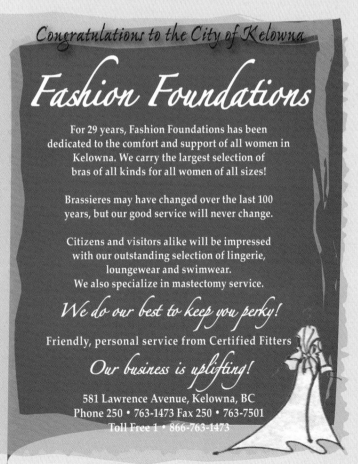
Canadian Pacific Airlines (CPA) began offering direct flights between Vancouver and Honolulu in the early '50s and Mernie joined thousands of other Westerners who escaped the long dreary winters and flew off to paradise. However, Mernie being Mernie, it wasn't long before her vacation turned into a working holiday when she discovered Alfred Shaheen, the major fashion designer in the Hawaiian Islands. Soon *Heather's* was stocked with his full line of denim outfits and when they sold out in a flash; Mernie knew she was onto something big.

By the following year, Mernie's Enterprises had been established and quickly became the exclusive Canadian agent for the Shaheen line, selling to Eaton's, The Bay, Olgivies in Montreal, and Holt Renfrew in Toronto. A year later, Mernie and Shaheen had a falling out but, undaunted, Mernie soon contacted Shaheen's competitors and convinced them she should represent all of them in a market she now had unique access to.

Never one to follow the norm, Mernie convinced Canada's department stores to offer summer clothes in the dead of the Canadian winter and they established the first of the now-familiar cruise wear departments in the process. Mernie was also the first to describe Kelowna as "Hawaii North "as she knew the summer tourists and visitors to the International Regatta and the Penticton Peach Festival would love her Hawaiian outfits.

It wasn't long before Mernie opened her first Hawaiian clothing store on the Penticton Indian Reserve near the airport. Only open during the summer, her *Grass Shacks* were modeled on the beach shacks which dotted the Hawaiian shoreline, complete with bamboo siding, tiki torches, and thatched roofs. A short time later, the Kelowna *Grass Shack* was opened at the west end of the newly opened Okanagan Lake Bridge. By the end of the decade, Mernie had opened more *Grass Shacks* in Radium Hot Springs, Kamloops, Nelson, Victoria, Prince George, Calgary, and West Vancouver. She was on a roll! Ever the marketer, it wasn't long before Mernie was able to convince an eastern ski shop operator to transform his winter stores into thatched-roofed *Grass Shacks* for the summer season which gave her additional outlets in Montreal, Toronto, Niagara Falls, Edmonton, and Vancouver.

The wholesale clothing industry was a tough place to break into in the '50s as high-pressure and usually hard-drinking eastern salesmen controlled the business. Mernie refused to conform and her mantra became "if you have to give up your femininity, you should get out of the business!" It wasn't long before Mernie had made her own unique inroads into the largely male-dominated industry.

Mernie's Enterprises was one of the first wholesalers to carry clothing for the entire family. With Heather as her on-the-spot model, Mernie charmed her way into the buyer's suites and, with her huge rolling racks of colourful merchandise, she showcased Hawaiian bathing suits, cover-ups, strapless summer dresses, and muu muus and then added in sandals, hats, purses, and jewellery. Matching outfits were also avaible for dad and the kids and the concept was such a hit and so unusual that it wasn't long before others in the industry incorporated her ideas into their marketing plans.

Mernie only thought on a grand scale and once talked Grant McConachie, President of CPA, into becoming her partner in presenting fashion shows across the country. The airline flew orchid leis from Hawaii across Canada in the freezing months of January and February, and as the models walked out of a mock-up CP cockpit onto the fashion runway in Mernie's brightly coloured Hawaiian outfits, newspapers across the country heralded the event as an industry first!

The Okanagan was party-central even in the '50s and Mernie gave some of the best on her thatched-roof houseboat – *The Grass Shack* – which glided around Okanagan Lake with her trademark tiki torches ablaze. A uniformed house boy looked after her elegant home on Abbott Street but since details were never Mernie's strong point, she eliminated the laundry room from her new home – even though her husband sold the appliances – because it was just easier to send clothes off to Henderson's Cleaners and have them take care of such mundane tasks for her.

A magazine cover photo of a pink Cadillac convertible belonging to the American boxer, Sugar Ray Robinson, caught Mernie's eye and she knew she had to have one. With her shocking pink cashmere sweater in hand, she went to McLean Motors in Vancouver and ordered the first-ever pink convertible in Canada. When the car arrived, crowds lined up four deep outside the dealer's showroom to gaze at the amazing sight.

Mernie wanted to live in the sun, wear beautiful clothes, have fun, and be successful – she was hailed as one of B.C.'s top business women in the '60s with one of the highest salaries in the province. She had many wonderful stories to tell and when she died in Kelowna in 2000, she had no regrets – after all – Mernie had truly lived her dream.

Regatta parade - circa 1950.

Kelowna Regatta

By Wayne Wilson

When Kelowna was incorporated in 1905, the citizens felt their community was established and economically stable. They also felt it offered its citizens the very best of social and cultural activities – seasonal and otherwise. Kelowna's Board of Trade brochure from about 1920 noted: *"Under the auspices of the Aquatic Association an Annual Regatta is held which is one of the great sporting events of the year and lends admirable impetus to the rivalry of canoeists, oarsmen, yachtsmen, swimmers and other aquatic experts."*

By far the largest percentage of Kelowna's citizens at the time were British by birth or British by descent; and one of that country's strongest traditions was the summer Regatta. What better way for those pioneers to help build some comfort about their new home than to start a new tradition - the Kelowna Regatta.

Beginning officially in 1906, George Rose, owner and editor of the Kelowna Courier and Okanagan Orchardist newspaper, is credited with the idea of a summer festival. When the Kelowna Aquatic Association Limited was formed in about 1909, Rose was elected its first President.

The Kelowna Regatta's first years were focused around boating and swimming events, and its competitors were largely local. Within three or four years, however, that all changed as the Aquatic Association raised funds to build a clubhouse in 1909 and grandstands to hold 800 spectators the following year. The revelry quickly built it into a two-day affair and, despite a modest slowdown during World War I, the grandstands needed to be expanded by 1920.

Through the 1920s, the Regatta drew increasing numbers of competitors from beyond the Okanagan Valley. Rowing crews from Nelson joined swim teams from Vancouver and power boat crews from Wenatchee, Washington. Another slowing of interest took place during the Depression of the 1930s, but World War II and the tourist boom that followed in '50s and '60s made up for it. In these decades, the Regatta parades got longer, there were more events, and the entertainment took on an international flavour.

Getting ready for the War Canoe Race.
Kelowna Regatta circa 1930.

The 1960s closed with a blow that almost killed the Kelowna International Regatta. In the summer of 1969, the Aquatic Centre and the grandstands burned to the ground and the spectacular event lost its home. Over the next years the Regatta events and activities moved from site to site, and in the 1980s were hit by two successive years of riots in the downtown area. Pulling together from these challenges, the Regatta officials have since re-focused their efforts to make the event an important part of Kelowna's summer schedule once again. In August each year an expanding array of fun-filled family events once again revolves around one of Kelowna's greatest assets – Okanagan Lake.

George Athans

&
Kelowna's Water Sport Family

Dr. George Athans in flight.

George Athans was Kelowna's two-time Olympic diver. First in 1936 in Berlin when he was 14 years old and later in 1948 in London. He was a British Commonwealth Champion in 1950 and an Olympic diving coach in 1960. He became the local co-ordinator during Regatta and attracted top divers from all over the world.

Irene Athans, George's wife, was the top Canadian Synchronized Swimmer and world titleholder for Masters Speed Swimming. She was a Canadian Champion and World record holder in Masters speed swimming.

George Jr. was two-time World Water Ski Champion.

Greg Athans was four time World Freestyle Champion and Canadian Water Ski Champion.

Gary Athans is a World Cup ski competitor and Olympic skier with Canadian titles in water skiing and snow skiing.

Photos courtesy of Gary Athans

23

Standing behind one of its products, Okay Port, the first principles of Domestic Wines and Byproducts Company, pose on the winery's loading dock. L to R: 'Cap' Capozzi, unidentified, W.A.C. Bennett, unidentified, unidentified, C.B. Ghezzi.

Okanagan Wines

By Juliana Hayes

An ad in a 1932 edition of the Kelowna Courier boasts: "From the world's finest fruit, Okay Wines." Even though the word "Okay" is intended as a reference to the Okanagan, this proclamation is not exactly a ringing endorsement. But if you were to consider today's standards, the term "Okay" would be a lofty compliment for the local wines of yesteryear.

Indeed, Okanagan wines have come a long way in the past 100 years. Their beginnings are humble, but rich in history, starting with plantings of Father Charles Pandosy, a French Oblate priest who established a mission in Kelowna in 1859. He recognized the area's potential for vineyards and his foresight has forever sealed his title as the father of the British Columbia wine industry.

But it is Guiseppe Ghezzi, a winemaker from Italy, who had the real vision when it came to the Okanagan wine industry. At the time, the Depression was having a devastating effect on the Valley's fruit growers who were struggling to get even a cent a pound for their apples. Ghezzi thought he could turn the apple crop into gold by using it to make wine. In 1932, he rounded up investors to start up a winery and later brought together two of Kelowna's most colourful characters, Pasquale "Cap" Capozzi, a well-known grocer, and W.A.C. Bennett, a hardware merchant, who served as

Premier of British Columbia from 1952 to 1972. They founded what was then known as Domestic Wines & By-Products Limited, the original name of Calona Vineyards, which remains as the province's oldest continually producing winery.

Ghezzi had the concept and the connections for getting the equipment necessary to start production. It fell to Bennett and Capozzi to raise the capital. They spent much of their free time traveling through Okanagan and Kootenay communities hitting citizens up for money and selling shares in the company at $1 a piece. They managed to scrape together $4,500, which considering the time and the fact that people were impoverished by the Depression, was no small feat. It was enough get them started and in 1932, Domestic Wines and By-Products was in business, operating out of an old concrete building adjacent to B.C. Orchards' new packinghouse.

The start-up of a winery created quite a stir in those days. The pages of The Kelowna Courier and Okanagan Orchardist were buzzing with news of the Domestic Wines & By-Products Limited plant. In an April 1932 edition, an article explains how local businessmen received a tour of the plant and were among the first to try some of the products being made.

"Among the samples of wines tasted by the visitors on Friday were beverages made from a mixture of Okanagan apples and Concord grapes, which blend to make a tasty wine and a palatable sauterne. Although not aged these wines compared favourably with others of a similar nature now being sold through the government liquor stores."

The Courier was being very generous in its remarks. In fact, the company readily admits the products were abominable. In its 50th anniversary publication, Calona Vineyards states: "The company's original apple wines – Okay Red, Okay Clear, Okay Port and Okay Champagne – were a bitter disappointment. Many bottles re-fermented on liquor store shelves and had to be thrown out. Liquor stores were reluctant to stock the ill-famed Domestic wines and people were reluctant to buy them. Sales for 1933 amounted to only a few thousand dollars, the company operated at a loss and no dividends on shares were distributed."

Within a few years, the name of the company had changed to Calona Wines Limited and it switched its focus away from apples to grapes. Still, Calona struggled as people then were barely able to afford food and clothing, let alone wine. The Catholic Church is the only reason why the company managed to survive. In 1935, a Kelowna priest named Father W.B. McKenzie suggested to the Archbishop that the church use Canadian products for sacramental wine rather than importing it from Spain.

The company grew incrementally over the years. Ghezzi eventually returned to Italy and married an opera star and his son Carlo took over the management. When he retired in 1960, Capozzi's three sons, Joe, Tom and Herb, grabbed the reins.

Over the years, Calona products have been a reflection of consumer tastes from the sweeter wines favoured in the 70s to the stylish vinifera wines preferred today.

An interesting episode in the company's history occurred in the 70s when the Capozzis almost convinced California's Gallo Family to become partners in Calona. That fell through and Calona was eventually sold to Standard Brands of Montreal in 1971. There have been several owners since, but it is now operated by Cascadia Brands.

Today, Calona Vineyards produces 70,000 cases of VQA wine sourcing grapes from 288 acres of vineyards in the Okanagan. It operates a second winery under the label Sandhill, a premium line of products that make up some 12,000 cases.

Calona may be the oldest continually producing winery in the Valley, but one of the oldest commercial vineyards in B.C. is actually located at another Kelowna winery – Pinot Reach Cellars. It was on these East Kelowna slopes in the mid 1920s that horticulturalist J.W. Hughes first planted wine grapes.

One of his foremen, Martin Dulik, eventually purchased some of his best vineyards and he and his son Daniel began replanting better quality varieties, including the much revered Johannisberg Riesling. Those vines, put in the ground in the early 80s, are among

the oldest vinifera grapes in the region and are used in Pinot Reach's highly-acclaimed Old Vines Riesling, introduced by Dulik's granddaughter Susan. Pinot Reach remained in the Dulik family for more than 60 years before being sold shortly after the devastating Okanagan Mountain Park fire forced the winery to dump its entire 2003 crop due to smoke taint.

In fact, the fire touched other Kelowna wineries in a very profound way, but none more so than St. Hubertus, located on Lakeshore Road. It was the only winery to sustain substantial structural losses when the wineshop, production facility and one of the owners' homes burned to the ground. Still, the Gebert Brothers, Leo and Andy, persevere and have since completely rebuilt. The vines, though the grapes that year were unsalvageable, miraculously survived to produce again in 2004.

The Geberts are no strangers to adversity. Immigrants of Switzerland, they purchased the St. Hubertus property in 1984, just in time to experience one of the Okanagan's coldest winters, for which they had to claim relief through crop insurance. But for the most part, the site has been good to them. The south western facing slopes benefit from the lake which moderates temperatures. The brothers replanted most of the site in the years since they first purchased the land and opened their winery in 1992. In the valley they are one of only two growers of Chasselas, a grape widely planted in their homeland and for which they have garnered a substantial following.

Neighbouring winery Summerhill Pyramid also opened in 1992 focusing mainly on sparkling and Icewines. But its reputation has been built less on its wines and more on the somewhat quirky initiatives of owner Stephen Cipes, a former New York City real estate developer. A devout environmentalist, Cipes was one of the first Valley vintners to adopt organic growing and winemaking techniques.

While other farms had grown grapes in the Kelowna area for decades, J.W. Hughes is the grandfather of commercial grape growning in the Okanagan Valley. The centre of his operations was located where one of Kelowna' premier family wineries stands today - St. Hubertus Estate Winery.

A little further east, is Cedar-Creek Estate Winery, which originated in the early 1980s as Uniacke. Like so many vintners in that time, Uniacke's owner set about replacing the less desirable labrusca varieties, planted in the early days of the industry, with respected vinifera vines. In 1984, Uniacke released a Merlot, the first of that varietal in B.C. Two years later, the winery was purchased by Ross Fitzpatrick, who has since been appointed a Canadian Senator. Under the direction of Fitzpatrick and his son Gordon, Cedar Creek has expanded substantially and has achieved a reputation as a top producer of Burgundian style wines.

Finally, House of Rose winery, which operates on a seven-acre section of land outside of Rutland, was opened in 1993 by Vern Rose, a retired school-teacher from Alberta. The property is a challenging site to grow grapes climate-wise as it does not benefit from the lake effect, being so much further inland. Rose has chosen to focus on cooler-climate varieties to compensate. The winery at press time was up for sale.

Probably taken in the 1950's, this photograph displays to trade show
consumers the full array of Calona Wines' product line.

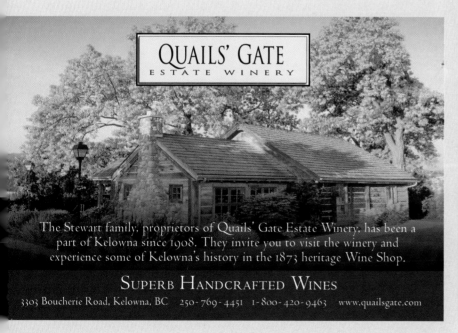

R. P. (Tiny) Waldrod at work as a chemist at Kelowna's Sun-Rype Products plant.

Kelowna's Renaissance Man
TINY WALROD

By Sharron J. Simpson

R.P. (Paul) Walrod was 6 4" tall and weighed 225 pounds when he was 14 years old – it was inevitable he would be called "Tiny" and the nickname stuck for the rest of his life.

Tiny's introduction to the Okanagan came during the Depression when he travelled to the Interior to pick grapes for his uncle, J.W. Hughes, the first commercial grape grower in B. C. Most of these grapes were being shipped to fresh fruit markets on the Prairies although Calona Wines in Kelowna and Growers Wine in Victoria were also buying Okanagan grapes for their wine production. The industry was in its very early stages and there was little of the refinement and quality control that is the hallmark of today's estate wineries – the screw-top gallon jugs of acrid 'plonk' showed little promise of what was to come.

While studying chemistry at university, Tiny spent his summers working for Modern Foods – the forerunner to today's well-known Sun-Rype Products Ltd. As the industry and company evolved and expanded, Tiny became the General Manager of both Sun-Rype and B.C. Tree Fruits Ltd., the industry's marketing agency. Travelling was part his job and he would always check out what was going on in other fruit-growing areas of the world: Could different crops be grown in the Okanagan? Could processing be done differently? What would enhance the Valley's fruit production? Tiny soon recognized the climatic similarities between the European wine-producing areas and the sunny dry hillsides at home, and he became an early advocate of the wine-growing potential of the Okanagan Valley. Tiny had other responsibilities at the time however, and while he often talked about a Valley wine industry, it was many years before he actively promoted the idea that wineries would be a great addition to the area's agricultural mix.

There was another side to Tiny which never appears in the stories about his involvement in the Okanagan fruit industry – he had an insatiable curiosity . . . about everything. Once, while doing business in New York City, he noticed a very attractive woman on the street corner. It wasn't so much the woman that drew his attention but rather the beautiful, vibrantly coloured coat she was wearing. Undaunted by the fact that he didn't know her, he approached, asked where she had purchased it and was amazed to learn that she had knit it herself. How did she do that? Where did she buy the wool? How long had it taken her? Did she need a pattern? Tiny returned home armed with all this information, found someone to teach him to knit and immediately began creating a replica of the beautiful New York coat for his daughter, Sharon.

Tiny's curiosity was unbounded and insatiable: he not only wanted to know how everything worked but how to do it himself, and if he didn't know he searched for someone to teach him. Another time he saw a beautiful ball gown in a magazine and wanted to know how such a stunning creation came to be. It wasn't long before Tiny figured out how to use a sewing machine and how to adapt a pattern to make it fit. He searched for a suitable fabric, learned the finer points of finishing and, in a very short time, created a stunning gown for his wife, Marie. It wasn't that Tiny wanted to become a seamstress, he just wanted to know how ball gowns came to be and once he had mastered that skill, he moved on to another interest.

Tiny had spent a lot of time with his grandparents as a young man and his grandmother – perhaps in lieu of a near-by granddaughter – taught Tiny to embroider and crochet. Many old timers can still picture Tiny waiting for his airplane in the airport lounge, quietly working on an intricate piece of embroidery, totally unconcerned – or perhaps unaware – that someone might think such fine hand work and this large, physically imposing, well-known businessman were a highly unusual combination.

Tiny was also an accomplished musician and people often commented that the man and his big double bass had, more-or-less, the same shape. Tiny played in the Charlie Pettman band during the late '40s and early '50s at the popular Kelowna Aquatic Club dances. When the dance was over, everyone would head off to Tiny and Marie's home on Pandosy Street where the jam sessions would continue late into the night.

Tiny had enormous amounts of energy to go along with his insatiable curiosity:

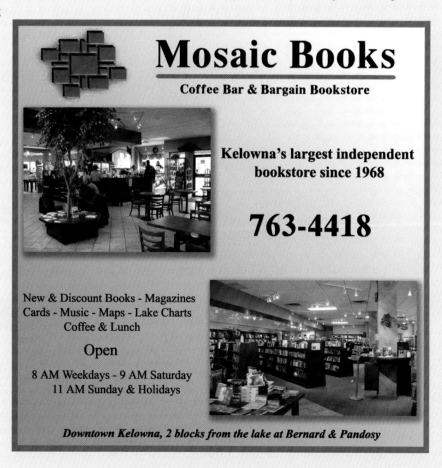

Along with everything else, he was also a proficient artist and nothing pleased him more than to be able to tuck an easel and canvas under his arm and head out to a vineyard or viewpoint to capture the beauty of the Valley's changing seasons.

Magic held special intrigue for Tiny and he befriended every magician who came to town. Tiny wanted to know why things happened the way they did and before long, he too became an accomplished hypnotist … until one day when he had difficulty retrieving his unsuspecting volunteer out of an hypnotic state and he quickly abandoned his amateur hobby.

Family, community, and professional activities were all an integral part of Tiny's busy life; he chaired the Kelowna General Hospital Board and the Canadian Horticultural Council, and in the midst of all this, managed to include his young daughter in his schedule without her realizing he was still working. Saturday mornings would find the two perched on the round stools at a local coffee shop, devouring a feast of toast and jam, before heading down to the Sun-Rype plant. Sometimes they would go to a movie and while waiting for the feature to begin, Sharon would write a list of 50 words and hand them to her dad who had 60 seconds to look at them before reciting them back to her – he rarely missed a word. They called it their brain game. While it was sometimes challenging to be attached to such a whirlwind, Sharon knew her dad always supported any venture she undertook.

In a succession of business decisions that seems curious in retrospect, Tiny ended his affiliation with Sun-Rype and B.C. Tree Fruits and was soon hired by a number of local businessmen who wanted to explore the possibility of establishing a Valley wine industry: The timing couldn't have been better as Tiny had long been a proponent of an Okanagan wine industry and Californian wines were just being introduced to world markets. Tiny visited California, learned about their start-up experiences, and returned to Kelowna to make a strong case for commercial grape production and an Okanagan wine industry.

As a result of Tiny's findings, Mission Hill Winery on Boucherie Mountain was opened in 1967. Its beginnings were rocky and in 1970 the winery's name was changed to Uncle Ben's Gourmet Wines Ltd. by its new owner, Ben Gintner, a brewer and industrialist from Prince George. The evolution of the Valley's wine industry from Uncle Ben's vintage – which must have been its undisputed low point – to today's Mission Hill Winery with its Tuscan bell tower, Chagall tasting room, and prize-winning vintages has typified the growth of the Valley's estate wines, and set the stage for the world-wide acclaim that has followed. Without Tiny's early determination and vision, today's wine industry and the unique way it showcases the Okanagan's natural surrounding and popular lifestyle would likely have taken a lot longer to come to fruition.

Unfortunately, Tiny never lived to see his vision become a reality. His abundant energy ran out one day in 1966 while he was peacefully painting his favourite view of Okanagan Lake. Tiny was a very young 56 years of age.

This is perhaps the earliest-known photograph of Kelowna. Taken in 1894, it shows all the attributes of a typical western town - false front buildings, wooden sidewalks, muddy streets, and hitching posts for horses.

Accommodation
IN AND AROUND KELOWNA

By Robert M. Hayes

Warm, comfortable shelter is a necessity of life. Clean water, food, warm clothing, companionship, and accommodation are paramount to survival. During the relatively short history of Kelowna and district, forms of accommodation have changed, reflecting the development of this part of the Okanagan Valley.

Prior to permanent white settlement, the First Nations in this region had their own type of homes. The "keekwil-lie", built partially underground, afforded warm dry housing in the Winter, and protection from the hot Okanagan Summer. So successful was this form of housing that at least one Okanagan pioneer, August Gillard, lived in his own keekwillie, apparently located somewhere near present-day downtown Kelowna.

There is much debate as to when the first white men actually settled in the Central Okanagan. In 1862, Isadore Boucherie, who lived near Mill Creek, unearthed the rotted log foundation of a large building, while he was clearing some of his land. These logs had been cut and shaped with axes or similar tools, and were of great vintage…the remains of much-earlier occupation, but a harbinger of later forms of construction.

The first permanent white settlement in the Central Okanagan occurred when the Oblate Fathers (Pandosy and Richard), Brother Surel, and their small entourage of settlers arrived in 1859-1860. The establishment of the Mission of the Immaculate Conception (popularly known as The Pandosy Mission) marks the beginning of continuous settlement in what was then known as the Mission Valley. Cyprien Laurence and his native wife Therese are credited with filing the first land claim, on December 15th, 1860. Settlement had begun.

The Lakeview Hotel was aptly named as it stood on Abbott Street at the foot of Bernard Avenue across the street from Okanagan Lake.

The pioneers of the 1860's through early 1880's lived relatively simple lives. Their homes reflected this simplicity. Constructed of logs, either squared or left round, these first Okanagan homes were generally small, usually with a room or two on the first floor, and sleeping accommodation under the pitched roof. The local McDougall family was considered the finest builders of log homes, and several of their buildings from the 1860's and 1870's are still extant, on the Pandosy Mission site, and also at Guisachan. Solid and uncompromising, and with little in the way of embellishment or decoration, these log homes served their occupants well, and kept them safe and warm on the Okanagan frontier.

With the passage of time, these simple log structures were often added to, or were covered with milled siding, giving them a more permanent and civilized look.

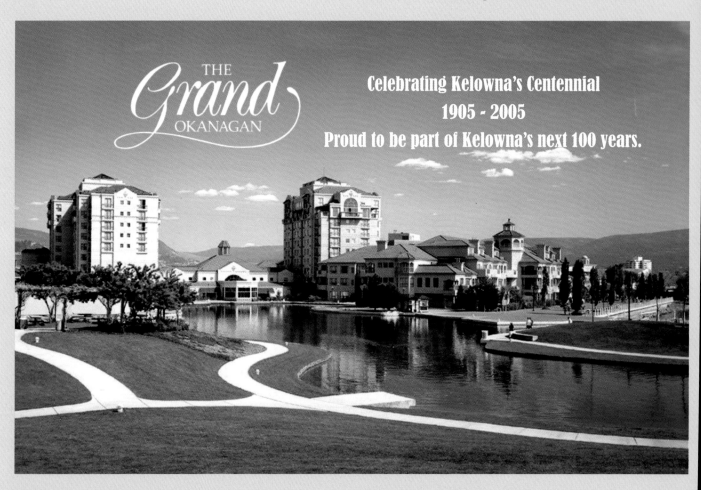

More settlement meant more people and industry, providing more materials for building. As early as the late 1870's, several sawmills were in operation in the Central Okanagan, providing finished wood for the building of newer and more commodious residences or for improving the look of the original log structures. The humble log cabin was considered out-dated, and a link with the uncivilized past. Sadly, many of these pioneer structures were destroyed or allowed to decay to nothing, as civilization advanced along the frontier.

THE WILLOW INN AND WILLOW LODGE, KELOWNA, B.C.

The Willow Inn Hotel and the Willow Lodge on Kelowna's waterfront combined a rustic charm with modern conveniences - all adjacent to the busy downtown core.

By the 1880's, the scattered population was growing, as more settlers arrived in the Mission Valley. Meanwhile, many of the bachelor pioneers – who worked at ranching, subsistence farming, or looking for gold on Mission Creek – were

sending "home" for wives, or married local native women. Families resulted, further adding to the burgeoning local population. Small log homes were clearly no longer adequate to house pioneer families, which frequently boasted a large number of children. The remaining log homes found new uses - as outbuildings, chicken coops, or barns - as the pioneers built larger homes, using milled lumber. The pioneer Whelan and Casorso families moved from their original log cabins into larger, more substantial Victorian and Edwardian homes, based on architectural styles from Eastern Canada, the United States, or England. The Valley was becoming more civilized, and this was reflected in this new style of accommodation.

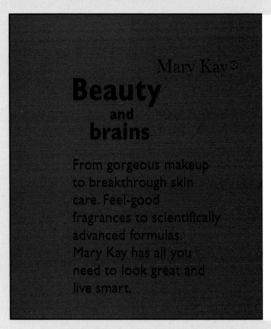

Of course, not all pioneers were able to erect large, expensive homes in which to ensconce their families. Rural areas around what would become Kelowna abounded with small, simple homes (some still made of logs), often inhabited by the men and women who found employment on the large ranches of the more successful pioneers.

The local population continued to grow, in the 1880's and into the 1890's, and it was inevitable that a town site be planned. In fact, two town sites were created, eclipsing the Mission (with its post office, general store, and hotel/bar run by the entrepreneurial and powerful Lequime family), and competing against the nearest town site, Vernon.

By the early 1890s, the days of the Okanagan cattle and land barons were fading. Land development companies were interested in dividing up the huge cattle ranches, creating smaller parcels for farms and orchards. The Central Okanagan was "open for business", as hundreds of smaller tracts of agricultural land were made available to the public. The region's population grew, as another wave of pioneers flocked into the Valley: farmers, orchardists, and would-be businessmen and women. It was no longer necessary

Kelowna's "Kumfy Kourt" was typical of the post World War II automobile tourist accomodation.

to make the arduous and time-consuming trip to Vernon, to pick up supplies. Two early 1890's town sites were laid out: Benvoulin and Kelowna.

Benvoulin had the advantage of being in the heart of the agricultural district, closer to Vernon, and in proximity to the Mission settlement. It boasted a few businesses, including a blacksmith shop and a small Tudor-style hotel. The latter establishment was an acknowledgement that more people were coming to the Okanagan, and they needed a place to stay, while investigating local economic prospects. Un-

fortunately, Benvoulin was too far from Okanagan Lake, fast becoming the Valley's main transportation system, so it faded into history. The Benvoulin Hotel has long since disappeared, while the historic church is one of the last physical reminders of that ill-fated town site.

Kelowna, however, flourished. Planned by Bernard Lequime and surveyed in 1892 by J.A. Coryell, Kelowna was originally but a few buildings strategically located on the lake-end of Bernard Avenue, close to where the lake steamer "Aberdeen" docked, unloaded its passengers and freight, and served as the crucial link with Vernon and the recently-completed Shuswap and Okanagan Railway.

One of the first buildings erected in Kelowna was the Lake View Hotel. Situated across from present-day City Park, this fine establishment provided comfortable accommodation for visitors and potential residents of Kelowna. The daily arrival of the SS Aberdeen (and later the "SS Okanagan" and "SS Sicamous") brought to Kelowna a steady stream of new citizens, speculators, and even a few early tourists. Many of these people stayed in the Lake View Hotel or the Palace Hotel which opened in 1905 on the north side of Bernard Avenue, a few blocks east of Okanagan Lake.

Kelowna's town site continued to grow, with small wooden stores on both sides of the wide main thoroughfare. Gradually, but steadily, the business section pushed eastward, and Bernard Avenue soon boasted a wide variety of stores and services, as well as some fine residences at its eastern end. Brick became a popular building material, often utilizing bricks made at the Kelowna Brickyard, at the foot of Knox Mountain. Some of these fine brick buildings remain, proud and tall, and reflecting the optimism which guided Kelowna's early residents. Carpenters such as Curts, Raymer, and the Clement brothers found ready employment, and built a variety of structures: businesses, small homes for the newly-arrived trades people and businessmen, and some of the larger homes for Kelowna's more successful and affluent citizens. A stroll up Bernard Avenue in the early years of the twentieth century was a pleasant one, and demonstrated that Kelowna was now nicely-established and destined to even greater things.

Meanwhile, outlying districts were growing. Rutland, Glenmore, Ellison, the Mission, South and East Kelowna continued to attract optimistic, hard-working new citizens from around the world. Agriculture was booming, and large commercial orchards, mixed farms, and the spin-off industries such as canneries and packing houses all needed workers. Although Kelowna remained the business centre of the district, communities sprung up around it, each carefully guarding its character and history. Early "bedroom" communities were developed, as Kelowna sought to expand its boundaries. The north end of Kelowna was opened up for housing – not the grand homes of an earlier era, but comfortable, affordable and practical abodes - with many of the new residents finding employment in local mills, businesses, orchards, and related industries.

Kelowna's character was changing rapidly. Large tracts of unused or agricultural land within the city limits were developed. The grand, impressive, Victorian homes of Kelowna's earlier business generation were replaced with smaller, less pretentious structures. In surrounding rural areas, land was further subdivided, as second and third generation family members "sliced off" their piece of the family farm or orchard. More homes were built, often surrounded by prosperous orchards, as settlement spread outward.

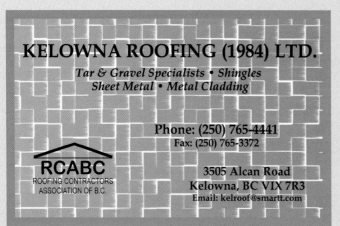

As Kelowna continued into the twentieth century, tourism became an important industry. The Okanagan's reputation for its healthy climate and beautiful scenery was spreading, as Kelowna became the chosen destination for Canadian and non-Canadian tourists. More hotels were needed. The impressive Royal Anne Hotel was built on Bernard Avenue, not to be outdone by the Willow Lodge and Willow Inn, located within the heart of Kelowna. The Mission boasted its own hotels: The Bellevue and The Eldorado. Small motels and "auto courts" sprung up along Lakeshore Drive, on Gordon (near Capri Centre), and strategically along other main entrances into Kelowna. The Franklin Motel, The Red Top Motel, The Inn Towner and The Glenmore Auto Court were four of the many popular haunts of tourists and their young families. Other visitors opted for the two downtown hotels, or the Capri Hotel which was erected in 1959 as part of the Okanagan's first shopping centre, then located in Glenmore, but subsequently a part of Kelowna's expanding downtown core. Kelowna's boundaries were being stretched, and this is certainly evident today with the proliferation of hotels, motels, strip malls and assorted eating establishments along Highway 97 North.

About 1946, with World War II ended, pieces of land were made available, at a favourable interest rate, to returning veterans and their families. The Bankhead V.L.A. subdivision of about seventy lots resulted, and small parcels of land (averaging one acre) were made available for the construction of homes for Canada's war veterans and their young families. Comfortable, yet practical homes were built, as the

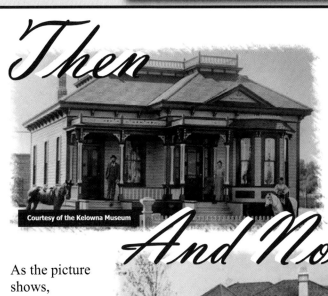

district's post-war population grew. Kelowna now had its own subdivisions, following the trend which was sweeping North America – suburbia. Fewer people worked in the agriculture industry, and more found lucrative employment in business, tourism, the trades, and service. Many of these people did not live and work on the same piece of property; they often lived in a subdivision or in-filled neighbourhood (as large chunks of Kelowna property were further subdivided and built on), and drove their cars to work. Kelowna was growing rapidly as it celebrated its Golden Anniversary of Incorporation, in 1955.

In September of 1960, parts of the Municipality of Glenmore were added to Kelowna, significantly increasing the city's area and population. As a result of this "boundary extension", Kelowna acquired large pieces of badly-needed undeveloped land. Urbanization of the Glenmore Valley has continued, with orchards and open fields replaced by subdivisions, gated communities, and small malls and business developments to serve the needs of the local residents. Amalgamation with Rutland and parts of the Mission, in early 1973, again dramatically increased Kelowna's area and population. Much of the formerly rural landscape of Rutland has been developed, to slake the city's thirst for more housing. While boasting its own business section and town site, Rutland has become another of Kelowna's bedroom communities, providing housing for the steadily-increasing population. The City of Kelowna has increased dramatically, as surrounding smaller communities have been absorbed.

As Kelowna grows, it faces many new challenges. An ongoing chronic shortage of land, pressures to develop agricultural land, and a steadily-increasing population necessitate a re-thinking of old ideas. High-rise buildings and urban towers such as The Grand Okanagan Lakefront Resort are now more acceptable. Previous notions of keeping Kelowna's "small town" look – with no buildings taller than a few storeys – are being challenged and discarded. Kelowna's skyline is changing, in reaction to the shortage of land,

The lobby of the Royal Anne Hotel in the 1930s. The painting of the Grizzly Bear in the background is now part of the Kelowna Museum.

continued increased demand for prime building locations, and the recognition that Kelowna is a city of more than one hundred thousand people. The First Nations' keekwillies, the primitive log cabins of the earliest pioneers, the Victorian homes of the prosperous ranchers and early business people, and the suburbia of mid-twentieth century have given way to the new "upward" architecture, as Kelowna moves into the twenty-first century.

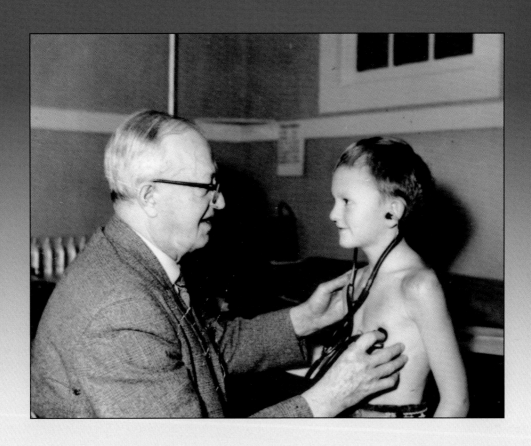

A Legend in His Own Time

DR. W.J. (BILLY) KNOX

By Sharron J. Simpson

Dr. William J. Knox first came to Kelowna in 1906 to fill in for the area's only doctor, Benjamin deFurlong Boyce, who was heading east for a six month refresher course. Billy, as he soon became known, was not long out of medical school and had been planning to see the world as the doctor on-board the S.S. *Empress of China.* However, when the opportunity came along to take over Dr. Boyce's practice and get some much-needed experience – and some money – Billy couldn't let it pass and decided to meet up with the *Empress* on her next call into Vancouver.

Small town Kelowna welcomed his arrival but at the end of his six month locum, Dr. Knox headed back to Vancouver to start his overseas adventure. Whether it was divine intervention or just small town good luck, the *Empress* was delayed three weeks and while he waited impatiently for its arrival, the restless Billy tossed a coin to decide whether to continue waiting for the ship or return to Kelowna and permanently join Dr. Boyce's practice. Kelowna won the toss.

Billy seemed to thrive and relish the adventures of doctoring the two thousand residents throughout the Okanagan. One story remains about a 49 year old mother in Naramata who was expecting twins, in urgent need of a doctor, and unable to wait for the S.S. *Aberdeen* to bring him on its regularly scheduled service. Billy received the message, left the party he was attending, scouted around town for Len Hayman, captain of the Kelowna/Westbank ferry, and the two putted down the lake as fast as their small boat would carry them. Billy arrived in time to assist in what turned out to be a relatively uneventful delivery, and since Len had a ferry schedule to keep, he dropped the doctor off and immediately returned to Kelowna … leaving Billy stranded at the south end of the lake for a couple of days, until the S. S. *Aberdeen* arrived at the Naramata dock on her regularly scheduled run and returned him to Kelowna.

Billy bought a car soon after returning to the Valley and while he was able to get around during the summer months, snow-covered roads in the winter and muddy bogs in the spring and fall, limited its usefulness. Besides, many of his patients didn't live by the roadside and a horse and buggy, a cutter in the winter, the regularly-scheduled sternwheelers to Peachland and Summerland, and row boats to Westbank all enabled him to treat patients wherever they were.

House calls were standard practice in those early days, although Kelowna's first cottage hospital was opened in 1905 by two English nurses, a larger community hospital opened in 1908 when Doctors Keller, Boyce, and Knox offered their services. However, many of the injured and sick couldn't be moved and it wasn't uncommon for a bed or dining room table to become an operating platform, with a few slugs of whiskey as the anaesthetic. While medicine progressed, it seemed that each improvement created its own complications. While attending a desperately ill patient who couldn't be moved, Dr. Knox used ether to knock her out during surgery … the only problem was that ether was highly flammable and since the patient's home was lit by gas lamps, the Doctor's car had to be driven up to the dining room window with its headlights turned up high to illuminate the dining/operating table while family members added their flashlights to areas where the headlights didn't reach. The patient recovered.

When Dr. Knox graduated from Queen's University Medical School in 1903, he didn't have the money to intern or specialize but he was always keenly interested in both new technology and medical research. Over the course of his practice he left the community, sometimes for weeks at a time, to upgrade his knowledge and skills. Always keen to improve his practice, Dr. Knox installed a new-fangled X-ray machine within a few years of its discovery to assist him in setting broken bones. However, little was known about the hazards of the new equipment and for the rest of his life, Dr. Knox suffered recurring skin malignancies on his badly burned hands.

Dr. Knox on his 80th birthday 1979.

While his colleague, Dr. Keller, restricted his practice to the English community, Dr. Knox treated whoever needed his assistance. Another tale remains about the Dr. being called out to an area north of Kelowna where a young lady of "easy virtue" had been dallying under a tree with an old timer. A young suitor arrived and warned the old man to desist … or he would shoot. Undeterred, the old timer carried on … so the young fellow fired a shot … and hit the young lady instead. By the time Dr. Knox arrived, the victim showed few signs of life. Undeterred, the doctor cut her hair along the wound line, decided the bullet had only grazed her skull, attached a piece of gauze to a probe which he then dipped in carbolic acid, and followed the path of the bullet along the edge of the bone. A few seconds later, the young lady let out a yelp, jumped up, and high-tailed it to a nearby cottage where she disappeared under the bed. It took some time for the good doctor to convince her to emerge so he could bandage the wound. She too recovered.

Billy Knox was a remarkable man and many who remember him say that his compassionate care, dedication to his patients, and his wonderful sense of humour were as much a part of their recovery as the potions he dispensed or the surgery he performed. He delivered over 5,000 babies in the area and was known to see three generations of the same family into the world. He had a phenomenal memory, never forgot a patient's name nor what had brought them into his office in the first place. His morning medical rounds at the hospital took on the air of a royal procession as gales of laughter and many smiles followed him around the wards.

Dr. Knox took his medical skills out into the community as the area's first Medical Inspector of Schools and, when he ran for a position on the School Board, he ended up with more votes than the mayor in the same election. In an era when everyone had to pay for medical care, Dr. Knox offered his services free to students whose parent's couldn't pay: the School Board acknowledged his contribution with the opening of the Dr. Knox Junior/Senior High School in 1961.

Knox was an enthusiastic lacrosse player, a member of St. George's Lodge, but his greatest passion, other than medicine, was politics though even the efforts of Mackenzie King, Canada's Prime Minister, couldn't entice the good doctor to give up his medical practice and accept a cabinet position in his government. Knox did, however, head up both the local and provincial Liberal associations.

Billy Knox became a much-beloved legend in his own time. Not only was he the consummate family physician but he was also a true friend to his patients. He was awarded the Order of the British Empire in 1948, an honorary LLD by his alma mater, Queen's University, and *Freeman of the City* by his adopted community. He practiced medicine in the Kelowna area for 60 years and his boundless energy, enthusiasm for life, and genuine care for those around him endeared him to everyone he encountered. He died in 1967, just a few days shy of his 90th birthday. All Kelowna had been blessed by his presence and all mourned his passing.

(The author is indebted to Dr. David Geen article in the 33rd Annual Report of the Okanagan Historical Society for much of the background information for this story)

Kelowna's first official hospital in 1908.

Frontier Health - 1908 Style

By the time of Kelowna's incorporation in 1905, there was already a serious community interest in providing professional medical services. Within a few years, that interest came to fruition with the construction of Kelowna's first hospital in 1908. Since then, the hospital has continued to grow with the community and with the advent of new technology and new approaches to medicine. A maternity ward was added in 1914; the hospital received accreditation in 1932; major additions built in the 1950s, 1960s and 1990s; as the 20th century closed a new cancer treatment centre was opened.

Dr. Boyce was Kelowna first resident medical doctor, moving here in 1894. Operating a pioneer medical practice took him up and down the Valley, but he soon focused his work in Kelowna. Joined by Dr. Knox and others in the ensuing years, these doctors found ready support in the community and practical help from well trained professional nurses who began training in Kelowna's own nursing school beginning in 1921.

At its Centennial, Kelowna's medical community is backed by wide ranging expertise and skills and by the most modern of technologies and procedures.

Prior to mechanization, apples were sorted, graded and packed by hand. Boxes of 'orchard run' fruit were gently dumped into a large canvas sling and the packers selected the size and quality of apples they needed.

Kelowna Industry

By Wayne Wilson

Looking back into Kelowna's industrial past, it becomes evident pretty quickly that there have been two large and distinct phases of development. In combination, this industrial growth has given Kelowna the useful and varied economic base that we enjoy today – one hundred years later.

The first forty to fifty years of Kelowna's growth turned around the rhythms and patterns of 'extensive agriculture'. That is, cattle ranching and grain growing carried the day – and the focus was clearly on raising "quantity", not "quality". The market for these cattle was the booming mining towns in the Cariboo, the Similkameen and in the Kootenay regions. And the nice thing about cattle for early Kelowna ranchers – they could walk to market.

That economic complex gave way to 'intensive agriculture' – orcharding – just prior to World War I. Though still strictly agriculture, this was a new economic order, and with that shift came the first wave of true industrial growth for Kelowna.

Between 1904 and 1914 thousands of acres of grazing land, hay flats and grain fields were planted to orchards. By the end of The Great War, that new acreage came in to bearing and, along with the rest of the Okanagan Valley, Kelowna

This rare photograph depicts some of the men who were instrumental in the shaping of our City.
Not only were these gentlemen heavily involved in the day to day business in the community,
setting the moral fiber and shaping a vision of what was to come, but they also
participated in the governing of the City as well.
The names are all recognizable from the history of City Hall.

welcomed an economic boom. The city's North End saw the construction of a supporting industrial base. Packinghouses, built along Ellis and Water Streets, handled increasing volumes of fresh fruit bound for domestic and foreign markets. In 1910 the Valley's packinghouses set out only a few hundred thousand boxes of apples. By 1928 that volume had grown to more than four million boxes. There was still a seasonal rhythm to life in Kelowna, but much of it was concentrated in the industrial North End.

Cold Storage buildings were often built adjacent to packinghouses and helped growers extend the selling-season for fresh apples and pears. Canneries added first-level processing of both tree fruit products and other agricultural produce. Box factories and growers supply warehouses rounded out the new economic order.

In addition to this industry, the more traditional occupations and trades were well-represented. Certainly the construction industry was booming – along with the industrial and commercial buildings came houses and churches and barns and more. Along the waterfront, boatloads of supplies were in constant transit and the local waterborne sawmill was in full production.

For the next forty years, this agriculturally based economy remained the driver behind most of Kelowna's employment. Improvements in transportation that came shortly after World War II and through the 1950s and 1960s, however, were harbingers of things to come.

The Hope-Princeton Highway opened in 1949 and finally offered Valley residents new and ready access to Vancouver. Equally important, it allowed the burgeoning Lower Mainland population access to Kelowna's growing tourist services. Okanagan Lake Floating Bridge was officially opened in British Columbia's centennial year, 1958. Finally, the Roger's Pass opened 1962 and ended Kelowna's isolation from the huge prairie market pretty quickly. While tourism development began to add a new complexion to Kelowna's growth, it was federal and provincial subsidies and incentives that brought tens of millions of dollars of industrial development to the area.

Beginning in the 1960s, two government programs brought international business focus to Kelowna and sparked the second wave of industrial development. The Department of Regional Economic Expansion (DREE) was joined by other similar programs to strengthen the agriculture sector and to improve the community

Kelowna's early cattle industry relied on cowboys to manage and drive the stock across the ranges and to market. Many of the ranchers hired men from the local Indian Reservation as cowboys and ranch hands.

This tobacco field, in full harvest, was located on Pandosy Street near the hospital. The plants were cut and a 'tobacco spear' was used to thread the stalks onto a wooden lathe for transport and drying in the tobacco barns.

Tobacco

By Wayne Wilson

One curious aspect of the pioneer experience in most colonial settings was the effort to experiment with almost every agricultural crop. Perhaps one of the most curious of crops in British Columbia was the trial and error cycle around tobacco growing. In the province, Kelowna was arguably the heart of that experimentation.

Within a couple of years of the townsite being laid out and named (1892), a pioneer named John Collins was growing tobacco in Kelowna and talking enthusiastically about its potential as a valuable cash crop. In the spring of 1895, Collins was joined by Louis Holman in an experiment to grow seven acres of tobacco on land leased from the Lequime family; it was a successful venture. By 1897 Collins had encouraged enough farmers to plant tobacco and a cigar factory was established at the foot of Bernard Avenue in what had been the Kelowna Shipper Union building.

Both Collins and Holman had a background in the tobacco business, and they found a ready market for their cigars in the booming mining towns of the Kootenay and Similkameen areas. Within a couple of years, however, the hardrock mining industry slowed and the tobacco and cigar industry fell apart with it.

The closing of this first cigar factory did nothing to dampen the spirits of local proponents of the industry. Collins, Holman and others gave lectures, attended agricultural fairs, and were boosters for the crop and its products. New little companies started up from time to time but generally they came to nothing. In December 1909, for example, Holman was behind the start of yet another company, The British Columbia Tobacco Company, Limited: *"The incorporation of this company forecasts the imminent great development of the tobacco industry in this district, and next season will see a large increase in the acreage devoted to this crop. The company is backed by some of the wealthiest men in Vancouver, and*

This tobacco field was located near Harvey Avenue and Richter Street with the owner of the Courier newspaper, George Rose, inspecting the crop. Tobacco can grow as much as 2.5 cm per day.

with the long experience of Mr. Lewis Holman – extending over a period of fifteen years – in coping with conditions of cultivation and curing in the valley, it starts its career under the most favourable auspices." (The Kelowna Courier and Okanagan Orchardist, 1910)

By 1912, their efforts attracted significant financial investment from the British North American Tobacco Company (B.N.A.T.CO.) and a new Kelowna company was capitalized at $500,000. The company built a substantial manufacturing plant on Ellis Street and at its height it employed 200 people. It was estimated the plant could produce as many as 25,000,000 cigars annually, but at its peak that figure was only around 800,000. The following year it was reported there were 500 acres planted to tobacco in the Kelowna area.

Though the company appeared to have a great start, it was short lived - to say the least. In May 1914, B. N. A. T. CO. was in liquidation as a result of mismanagement, some shady dealings and a world depression that began in 1913.

After World War I, there was another flurry of interest in the crop. Aided by scientists at the Summerland Research Centre, the new crops were shipped to the Coast for processing with tobacco grown in the Sumas area. The Canadian Tobacco Company made largely pipe tobaccos but it also produced some cigarette tobaccos. In 1929 Kelowna boasted about 100 acres in tobacco crops.

The Great Depression of the 1930s brought another slump in the industry, and tobacco growing never did recover. Plagued with a number of problems from the beginning, tobacco was probably destined to fail in Kelowna. First, by very shortly after 1900, the tree fruit industry had a strong foothold in the entire Okanagan Valley. Second, and perhaps most important, Canadian national tariff problems resulted in British Columbia growers having to charge a premium for their tobacco and, as a result, raise the price of their cigars, and the market fell apart as a result.

What is left is an intriguing part of the community's past – a past that is replete with a spirit that will try, that will experiment, and that will try again. And, of course, there are the artifacts, now collector's items that help tell that story.

Stanley M. Simpson being granted *Freedom of the City* by Mayor J.J. Ladd at a Civic
Dinner in 1957 in recognition of his efforts to enhance the city. Dr. Billy Knox, a
well-known medical pioneer, is in the background.

An Unlikely Success
STANLEY M. SIMPSON

By Sharron J. Simpson

Stan Simpson wrote a letter to Kelowna's Mayor J.J. Ladd in May of 1957 thanking him – and the City – for the honour of being granted the *Freedom of the City*. Stan's letter went on to say that he was filled with "a sense of humble gratitude … and he would treasure the honour as one of his most cherished possessions."

The civic dinner which acknowledged Stan and his contributions to the community was attended by over three hundred local and out-of-town dignitaries, and was a very grand occasion in comparison to Stan's unheralded arrival in the small town, 44 years earlier.

When Stan disembarked from the sternwheeler, S.S. *Okanagan,* to look into buying a small carpentry shop just off Kelowna's main street, it was to be the end of a nine year odyssey across Canada. From Chatsworth, Ontario, where he had grown up, Stan had travelled to Toronto and worked as a carpenter for a few years before joining the wave of settlers heading west, in 1906, to settle the Prairies. Though he had never farmed, Stan tried homesteading for the next three years before realizing his carpentry skills offered a better chance for making a living than the 160 acres of scrub-covered prairie.

Stan and a partner bought the carpentry shop and began making screen doors that were guaranteed not to sag, storm windows, orchard ladders, and custom Christmas toys for those who could afford them – which Stan then loaded into his wheelbarrow and delivered around town.

Though his partner abandoned the business when hard times descended on the community during WWI, Stan remained optimistic and managed to keep working by doing whatever needed to be done – often charging his customers 10¢ or 25¢ to repair a broken pipe or sharpen a saw blade.

"If you can't afford to pay cash, eat porridge until you can" was one of Stan's favourite mottos and as he watched his pennies grow, his business also grew and soon after the end of WWI, he was able to move to larger premises. By this time the volume of produce from the Okanagan's orchards and market gardens had grown substantially and demand for the wooden boxes Stan had recently started making had also increased.

In fact, Stan's business grew so much that he needed greater production capacity and just as the Great Depression was about to descend on the country, he built a sawmill and box factory at Manhattan Beach, in Kelowna's north end – which, at the time, seemed to be a long way from the town's Bernard Avenue business district. Stan also saw an opportunity to provide the orchardists and market gardeners with a greater variety of wooden containers and built the first veneer plant in the Valley.

S. M. Simpson Ltd. struggled through the Depression and even when he had no orders, Stan kept some parts of the plant operating to provide a few jobs for the men who congregated around the mill office in hopes of getting a few hours work. If he had no money to pay them, Stan told them to go to the grocery store and charge what they needed until they had some money to pay the bill – and he would guarantee their debt – it's unlikely he ever had to pay.

However, in September of 1939, World War II was declared and the country's economy did a quick turn around. The unsold lumber that had been stacked over much of the mill yard quickly vanished with the sudden demand for any available wood, and S.M. Simpson Ltd. became a critical wartime supplier. Stan spent the next five years manufacturing wooden boxes for the British Box Board agency and shipping them to Britain and India, as well as continuing to supply boxes to the Valley's orchardists.

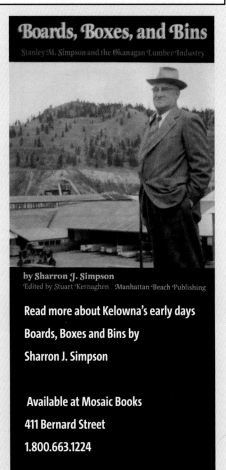

Building Dreams For 30 Years

LA PORTA DEL LUSSO
Winner of Regional & Provincial Awards

Excited for the Future

Taking us into the future with new homes in the
KETTLE VALLEY subdivision

Stan further expanded his sawmill operation in the early '40s by purchasing the Kelowna Saw Mill (KSM) from pioneer, David Lloyd-Jones. Several acres of prime land on the edge of the Bernard Avenue business district had been occupied by this lumber operation since the late 1890s, and when the sawmill was destroyed by fire in 1944, Stan decided not to rebuild. With his sawmill operations consolidated at Manhattan Beach, Stan offered the old mill site's 11.2 acres to the City of Kelowna for use as a civic centre for what amounted to the cost of clearing the fire debris from the site – which was, even at the time, a modest sum. This is the location of today's Kelowna City Hall, the Kelowna Museum, and the Memorial Arena and several other government buildings which have subsequently been demolished.

During the mid '40s and throughout the '50s Stan had his differences with the aggressive recruiting tactics of The International Wood-workers of America (IWA). He became the industry spokesman and was adamant and immoveable about protecting the mill workers' right to choose whether they would join the union or not – or have union dues automatically deducted from their pay cheques. The resulting labour disputes became legendary in their duration and animosity.

During this time, the fruit industry decided to switch to corrugated cardboard containers and away from the costly, heavier wooden boxes, and S.M. Simpson Ltd. began searching for better ways to use the area's forests. In 1957, S&K

Plywood Ltd. was up-and-running and, after designing and producing the first plywood bulk bin, went into full production of what has now become a worldwide industry standard.

The demands of wartime, years of confrontation with the IWA, and little time off, finally took their toll on the quiet, unassuming businessman. Stan suffered a major stroke in 1955, when he was 69 years old, and retired from the company to which he had devoted most of his working life.

When the city choose to honour Stan with the *Freedom of the City* two years later, he was truly "at a loss to understand why I should be chosen" for the honour.

What the city didn't know at the time was that, upon his death in 1959, Stan would establish the Knox Mountain Trust to provide for improvements to the public park overlooking downtown Kelowna. In 2003, the balance of the Trust was finally spent, in partnership with the City, to build the beautiful Pioneer Pavilion, caretaker's residence, and public facilities on the top of Knox Mountain.

Stan compensated for his lack of book-learning with determination, unwavering principles, and a willingness to take risks. During his lifetime, Stan's tiny carpentry business evolved into the Okanagan's largest year-round employer, but if someone had interviewed this shy, retiring young man as he walked down the S.S. *Okanagan's* gangway in the summer of 1913, it's highly unlikely they would have marked Stan to become the successful, innovative businessman he eventually became. Nor would they have seen any signs that he would have had the wisdom or resources to be able to leave such a generous legacy to his adopted community.

Glenmore School site was selected in 1912 just as the orchard lots of the Central Okanagan Land Company were coming on the market.

School Days

by Colleen Cornock

Father Charles Pandosy and Father Pierre Richard established the first, private school in the Okanagan region at the Immaculate Conception Mission. As greater numbers of pioneers settled in the Okanagan Valley there became a need to establish certain amenities such as a school. Thus, the Oblate Missionaries established a private, one-room schoolhouse on the Mission property. In 1863, five children were recorded as attending the school, receiving their education in the French language. One can imagine that the Oblate Missionaries would have been considerably busy, managing their teaching duties as well as their other responsibilities - including raising livestock and grains, and performing religious duties such as baptisms, marriages and funerals.

The priests were able to maintain these duties as well as teaching until approximately 1866, when, according to records, the operation of the school ceased. While the reason for the closure is unknown, some have suggested that the Missionaries where overwhelmed with their additional responsibilities. This may have been the reason if the priests were the only teachers onsite; however, this was not the case. Swiss-born Joseph Buchman was teaching at the Mission in 1865 and remained there for approximately twenty-seven years. One should look, therefore, to another possible reason for the school's closure. The closure may stem from the arrival of more settlers into the region, thus facilitating a need for the creation of a larger educational facility.

It would be eight years before a public school was opened in the area. In the interim, settlers were forced to home-school their children, or have them attend schools at the Coast.

In 1872, the Province's first Superintendent of Education, John Jessop visited the Okanagan to examine the Valley's educational system; he found no school. In 1874, Jessop returned to the Valley and met with settlers in an effort to

C H R Y S L E R

Parker's Chrysler Dodge Jeep

1946

Parker Motors was opened in 1946. It is one of the oldest family owned car dealerships in BC.
It was opened by Glady, Lloyd and Gordon Parker in the old Nanaimo and Winnipeg Street location.
In the early days, they could only get about twelve to fifteen new cars a year.
Customers would line in up to sign for a new car. The car business was so small Parker started
selling tandem trucks, tractors and bulldozers.
They were from the US and were reconditioned from being in the war.
Much of it came from Okinawa, Japan. All the factories had been tooled to help
the war effort so normal car production was put on
hold until after the war ended.

1953

In 1953 Lloyd Parker took part of the business and opened
Parker Industrial, now known as Inland Kenworth.
Gordon and Glady Parker built the current building and
relocated there in 1969.

1973

Chris Parker came into the business in 1973 and took over for Glady
and then bought his Dad out in 1978. Chris ran the business until his death in 1996.
Janet Parker, his wife, became President at that time and continued with the Parker tradition.
Their son Colin is currently at the dealership and will continue on in the family business.
Colin also wants to continue on in providing excellent
product and service to Parker's customers.

2005

Parker Motors is planning to expand the showroom and renovate parts of the existing building.
We are also upgrading systems to better serve their customers.
In addition, we are opening up a business that will feature all make accessories,
performance enhancements and a larger detailing department.

*The Parker family and their employees look forward to
continuing to meet your automotive needs.*

Parker Motors Ltd.

A Name You Can Trust Since 1946

250.492.2839   1.866.492.2839

www.parkerschrysler.com

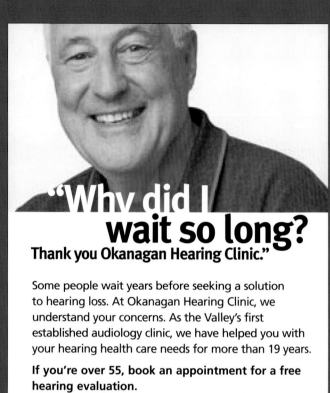

Past, Present and Future

KI-LOW-NA FRIENDSHIP SOCIETY

Ki-Low-Na Friendship Society

Over 30 Years of Community Service

Provides support for the mental, emotional, physical and spiritual well-being of all peoples through the development of community-based services, while encouraging the community to preserve, share and promote Aboriginal cultural distinctiveness.

encourage the establishment of a school district. His efforts paid off; on July 31, 1874, the Okanagan School District was created. The Okanagan School District, centered in the Mission Creek region, served approximately twenty-four children.

The district's first public school, the Okanagan School, was built on an acre of land donated by William Smithson. The school was situated in what is now considered Benvoulin near the current School District # 23 Board Office. The school served children in the surrounding area as well as those from other regions of the Valley boarding with local residents. The school was ready by 1874, but did not open until December 1875; the district had great difficulty attracting a teacher. Eventually, Angus McKenzie accepted the posting, and supposedly arrived in the Valley by foot, carrying his books and blankets on his back. McKenzie, a native of Pictou, Nova Scotia, earned a first class certificate from Kansas and was considered a hard working, conscientious teacher. While employed at the Okanagan School, he earned a salary of sixty dollars per month, which was supplemented with goods such as butter, milk and meat, given to him by the settlers. Though he was known for his dedication as a teacher, he also served as orator during any Sunday services that the minister was unable to attend. McKenzie remained at the school until 1878.

In 1878, Miss N. Coughlin replaced McKenzie as teacher at the Okanagan School. According to one of Coughlin's students, William Brent, the teacher's interest in Catholicism was often expressed in her daily teachings at the public school. If we look to Brent's unpublished, handwritten *History of the Okanagan Valley,* we are provided with a suggestion as to how the teacher's desire to incorporate Catholicism into her teachings may have resulted in the end of her tenure in 1882.

According to Brent, Coughlin's focus on Catholicism in the classroom became a contentious issue for some Protestant parents. Upon learning of this over emphasis on religious teachings from both his son and fellow parents, Frederick Brent, a Trustee for the Okanagan School, took action. Frederick Brent decided to close the school until he could arrange for a suitable replacement teacher. According to William Brent's unpublished account, on the day his father chose to close the school, Father Pandosy was in attendance. Brent states that as his father closed the school, Father Pandosy turned to him and said with a smile "You bad man". Fredrick Brent's goal of hiring a teacher that would place less emphasis on Catholicism was achieved when he hired Mr. R.S. Hanna, a Protestant. According to William Brent, his father was once again plagued with the issue of religion in the classroom when he found Hanna reciting Protestant hymns which he intended to incorporate into his lesson plans!

Religious issues aside, the original school remained operational until 1906, when the log building was torn down and replaced with a new one-room school. Until 1929, the Okanagan School operated under its original name, when it was renamed the Benvoulin School.

When the Oblate Missionaries came to the Okanagan in the 1860s, they believed future townsite development would occur in the area surrounding Mission Creek. The Mission was the site of a church, a homestead and a school; it was the early centre for activity. Despite this early development by the Oblates, by the 1880s, the focus of town site development turned to the area surrounding Lake Okanagan. Early pioneer, Bernard Lequime, recognized early on the importance of Okanagan Lake to townsite development. Lequime knew the Lake would facilitate transportation routes to other areas in the Valley and, as such, he made arrangements to acquire waterfront property and began to map out plans for a townsite. On August 13, 1892, Bernard and his brother, Leon Lequime, filed Map 462, the Townsite of Kelowna with the Registrar General in Victoria. Soon after the plans were drawn, building began and resulted in the construction of Kelowna's first general store and public school.

The Lequime General Store had been built with a hall above it; this 24x30 one room hall would serve as Kelowna's first public school. The school was opened on January 1, 1893; D.W. Sutherland was employed as the school's first teacher.

The small hall was used as a school until the summer of 1893, at which time a new school was constructed near the corner of Ellis Street and Queensway. The new building would not only serve as an educational facility but, after school hours, Mr. Sutherland would also hold court as Justice of the Peace.

In the early 1900s, Kelowna experienced a growth in the number of public schools. In 1904, the Board School (Brigadier Angle Armory), located on the northeast corner of Richter Street and Glenn Avenue, served as an elementary school. A few years later in 1910, the High School was built on the southeast corner of Richter Street and Glenn Avenue (now Lawrence Avenue).

According to an article by F.T. Marriage in the *18th Report of the Okanagan Historical Society, 1954,* by 1925, this six-room brick structure was "staffed by only three academic and one agricultural teacher". The number of students in the area grew rapidly and in order to accommodate increasing numbers, a new elementary school had to be constructed. Until completion of the new Kelowna Elementary School (later known as Central Primary), elementary and secondary students attended the High School.

Finally, in 1913, Kelowna Elementary was completed with ten classrooms. The building, which is still in use, is located on Richter Street two blocks

south of the former Kelowna High School. By 1925, the number of high school aged students increased to a point where it was necessary to hire four additional teachers for the High School. By 1929, necessity led to the construction of the new Junior High School. Fifty-four years after the small one-room school opened above the Lequime store, Kelowna had established an expansive, secondary educational, facility complete with seven classrooms, library, home economics department, woodwork shop, gymnasium and a four hundred seat auditorium.

Central Elementary School was built in 1913 but officially opened in early 1914. It is arguably the city's most distinct piece of public school architecture.

In 1939, an addition was built on the Junior High School. This red brick structure accommodated senior high grades and since its construction has become a focal point in the landscape of Kelowna's downtown. Though the original Junior High School portion of the impressive Richter Street structure was used only until 1979 (tragically it was destroyed in a fire), the Senior High School portion remained in operation December 2001.

While the number of public schools in the downtown core grew, so too did the number of schools in outlying areas. In 1893, in the area now known as Rutland, residents opened the area's first school. Black Mountain School was located on the property of local resident Jim McLure. It was a small log cabin on the northeast corner of what are now Belgo and Lewis Roads. Local residents assisted in the building of the structure and when completed it served children of eight families. Many children were faced with tremendous distances to travel in order to attend the school, some walking as many as seven miles.

The residents of the community of Ellison, like their counterparts in Rutland, came together to build their community's first school. In 1894, one year after the Black Mountain School opened, Ellison residents realized that their population had increased to a level that warranted the building of a public school. Land donated by George Whelan enabled settlers to build the Okanagan Mission School (renamed Ellison School in 1908), the fourth school to be established in the Okanagan Valley. As a small rural school, Okanagan Mission School faced the on-going challenge of remaining in operation, failure to maintain an adequate number of students; combined with minimal funding grants from the Department of Education were constant threats to the future of the school.

In 1911, residents of North Glenmore established their first school. The community recognized the need for a school as it was too far for children to walk from Glenmore to Kelowna. As in many other rural areas in the Valley, the schoolhouse was a one-room cabin, donated by a local resident and converted to a schoolhouse. North Glenmore grew as a community and in 1912; the area created its own school district entitled "North Kelowna".

Whether it was in Kelowna, Rutland, Ellison, North Glenmore, Peachland, Oyama, or Southeast Kelowna, school districts emerged independently of one another. In each area, schools developed as more children of school age moved into an area, residents

Ellison School operated from 1895 - 1911 and was built on land donated by George Whelan.

came together to establish much needed educational facilities. I would not be until 1945 that the Provincial Government would request an inquiry as to the existing system of school district throughout the province.

Until 1945, areas throughout British Columbia including the Okanagan Valley consisted of city school districts, rural schools districts and district municipality school districts. Throughout the Province, schools experienced inequalities with regards to funding received and education levels provided. In 1945, Maxwell Cameron was ordered by the Province to investigate the situation of school districts and as a result produced the Cameron Commission Report. The result of this report was the creation of larger school districts, rather then numerous smaller districts.

Today, School District #23 spans from Peachland to Oyama, includes twenty-nine elementary, six middle and five secondary schools. The District is comprised of approximately 22,000 students and approximately 1,200 educators. From its humble beginnings of a one-room public school on the top floor of the Lequime General Store with twenty-nine pupils to a district of forty schools and 22,000 students, Kelowna and District has certainly seen growth, development, and opportunities for the residents of the Central Okanagan.

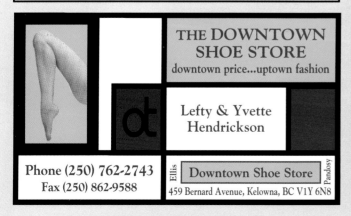
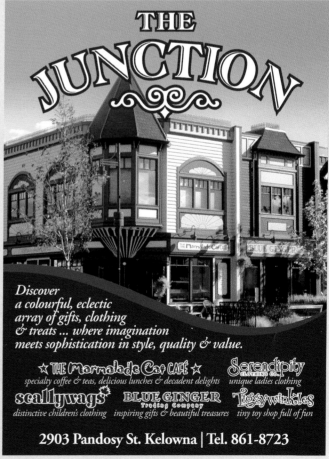

Cattle ranching was Kelowna's primary economic activity during the settlement era. This photo, from about 1905, shows the extent of grazing land on the A.B. Knox ranch in Kelowna's North end.

Which Knox Was it Anyway

THE NAMING OF KNOX MOUNTAIN PARK

By Sharron J. Simpson

Two men figured prominently in the history of Knox Mountain Park. The first, Arthur Booth Knox, was a convicted felon. The second, Dr. Benjamin deFurlong Boyce, was the first medical doctor in the area and widely known for his benevolent civic-mindedness.

Knox, a Scot, arrived in the Okanagan late in 1874, via the Cariboo gold fields. He purchased 4,000 acres of land on the Valley bottom adjacent to the soon-to-be-surveyed town site of Kelowna. Through a Crown grant, he also acquired the land from Manhattan Beach northward along Okanagan Lake to Okanagan Centre and Winfield, including the mountain which bears his name.

Arthur Knox was known either as "a hardworking, industrious man" or a vengeful self-serving arsonist who went to great lengths to ensure his own financial well-being.

In 1890, the whole Valley was caught up in the hay burning scandal. Tom Ellis, a prominent rancher whose empire extended from Okanagan Mission south to the U.S. border, accused Knox, the area's other land and cattle baron, of setting fire to his three prize – and very valuable – haystacks. It seems there were too many cattle in the Valley for the amount of hay that was available and the torching of 200 tons of Ellis's hay was seen, at least by Ellis and his supporters, as Knox's solution to ridding the areas excess cattle by starving them to death and thus wiping out his competition. Many witnesses were called to the Vernon County Court, a number of who were known to be unreliable and later admitted to being bribed – by both the defendant and his accuser. In spite of his protestations of innocence, Arthur Booth Knox was found guilty and ordered to serve three years at hard labour.

Two years later, in a curious follow up, Tom Ellis went to court in an attempt to force the arsonist to reimburse him for his losses - $4,000 for his first class timothy hay destroyed by fire, $500 for the resulting underfed cattle, and repayment of the reward Ellis had paid to the witnesses who had appeared against Knox.

The Court was not amused, saying the previous trial had no bearing on the current trial and without further evidence that Knox was at fault, the jury found against Ellis who then had to pay the court costs of his unfortunate action. By this time, Knox had pretty well served his full term at hard labour and returned to Kelowna upon his release from jail. Perhaps in an attempt to redeem himself, Arthur Booth Knox donated land to the Presbyterian Church on the corner of Bernard Avenue and Richter Street (now First United), in 1896. Five years later he was elected president of the prestigious Agricultural and Trades Association and worked, along with several prominent citizens, to promote the area's produce to the outside world.

As Kelowna grew and the land development companies bought up the vast cattle ranges, Knox sold his ranch to the Okanagan Fruit and Land Company for $75,000. The land was subsequently subdivided into both residential and orchard properties, while Knox's upper ranch land, including what was to become Knox Mountain Park, was sold in 1906.

Arthur Booth Knox never married and died in Kelowna in 1925. He left a very considerable estate and no will – relatives in Scotland were the eventual beneficiaries.

Dr. Benjamin deFurlong Boyce arrived in Kelowna in 1894, from the mines in Fairview. For years he was the only doctor between Vernon and the U.S. border but he was also an entrepreneur rancher in what is now downtown Kelowna and the Benvoulin area, and operator of a small sawmill on the lakeshore (now Kinsman Park) where his family used the adjacent beach as their summer camping grounds.

Boyce was the doctor to many: the prisoners-of-war interned at the Vernon army camp and the army personnel stationed there, the communities throughout the Valley, as well

as the unemployed single men who were sent to the National Defense camp at Wilson's Landing, on the west side of Okanagan Lake, during the Depression. He was also both doctor and advocate for the native peoples in the area.

Dr. Boyce and his wife, Mary, didn't have a family and generously donated land to various groups including part of the old Kelowna Senior Secondary site to the Kelowna Lawn Tennis Association, Boyce Gyro Park as a public picnic and bathing beach, and other lands to different churches. In 1912, Dr. Boyce bought the 190.82 acres of land on Knox Mountain and in 1939, sold it as parkland to the City of Kelowna for $1.00.

Dr. Boyce died in 1945 and his generous donation to the city is acknowledged on a dilapidated cairn at the top of Knox Mountain.

A second cairn acknowledges Stanley M. Simpson who, upon his death, established a trust fund for capital improvements to the Knox Mountain Park. The first expenditure was to make the area more accessible by paving the road to the top of the mountain, and the second was for the construction of the Stanley M. Simpson Nature Pavilion.

By 2002, a substantial amount of money remained in the Stanley M. Simpson Trust and, at the request of his descendents, the balance was combined with funds from the City and the original nature pavilion was replaced with a much grander building. It was also renamed The Pioneer Pavilion, to acknowledge the contribution of the area's many pioneers. A caretaker's residence and public facilities were also added to the site.

Kelowna had two men by the name of Knox who were prominent in its early years. One, Dr. W.J. "Billy" Knox was a well-respected doctor whose compassionate care is still remembered. The other,

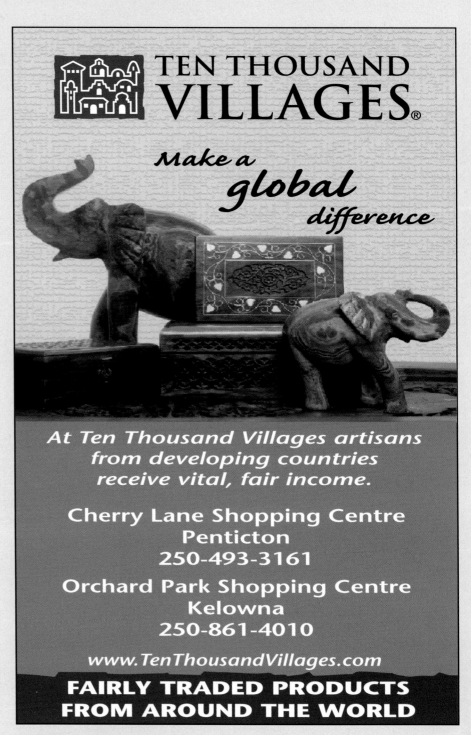

Arthur Booth Knox, the original owner of the Knox Mountain property, whose reputation was tainted by a criminal conviction, is the Knox the mountain is named after. A small plaque noting this fact has been placed near the Boyce and Simpson cairns at the top of the mountain – small, not obvious at first glance, but at least acknowledging the existence of the original – if somewhat wayward – property owner.

Kelowna's North End sports focus has been evident since incorporation in 1905. About 1910, part of that focus was an active race track complete with corrals and grandstands.

The Sporting Life

By Wayne Wilson

From the neighbourhood game of scrub baseball to the Memorial Cup in 2004, sports have been an important and exciting part of Kelowna's history. Early in that history, the sports events were informal to say the least. There were no arenas, no badminton halls, no curling rinks – but that certainly did not hold the pioneers back. If there ever was an example of necessity being the Mother of Invention, Kelowna's settlers embodied that spirit wholeheartedly. Horse races between the Okanagan Mission and downtown Kelowna drew cheering crowds; curling matches on the local ponds tightened community ties and spoke of cultural connections an ocean away; and hockey games on the frozen shores of Okanagan Lake brought fun and frivolity for all.

Kelowna's North End has, since incorporation in 1905, been a focal point of team and individual sports. Strings of polo ponies raced across the flatlands and gave the new community a sense of connection to Great Britain where many of the pioneers came from. An oval horse race track was laid out and graded in the same area as the Polo field, and drew crowds from up and down the Valley. A little closer to the downtown, the first Golf Course was laid out in the area near the Laurel Packinghouse.

Today, Kelowna's North End maintains an important sports focus for the City. King Stadium was named for Willie King, who spent countless hours promoting amateur baseball for both boys and girls. Its baseball stadium and other ball diamonds were given a huge boost by the Kelowna Elks Club. The club had thrown its support behind the Kelowna Stampede in the north end around World War II, but they switched their focus shortly after that and got behind the development of the area as the "Premier Sports Centre" in the Interior of the province. The area is complimented by other sports facilities too. A curling rink was built in 1978, and the Badminton Hall was constructed. Even the name "Recreation Avenue" gives a pretty clear hint about the area's history.

Kelowna's downtown City Park has been and remains a showcase for many different sports. While the Regatta and its swimming, diving and boating events might be remembered first, the park has been home to everything from rugby, soccer and cricket to tennis, beach volleyball and lawn bowling. Perhaps one of the Park's most enduring sports has, indeed, been lawn bowling. This sport has been played in Kelowna since at least 1909, and it got its greens and clubhouse in City Park in May 1940. Today, almost every park within the city limits is host to some sort of sporting event.

An enduring place in this line-up is Kelowna's connection to hockey. Played avidly on local ponds and on the lake's frozen shores, the first big step forward for hockey in Kelowna was the construction of the Memorial Arena. Opened on Remembrance Day in 1948, the building quickly became synonymous with outstanding hockey talent. That greatness came to the forefront in 1958 when the Kelowna Packers, who called the Memorial Arena home, travelled to Russia. In November that year they handily defeated the Russian Select Team 5 – 1. Such a boost was all Kelowna needed, and since then its young and talented teams have gone on to win dozens of Divisional, Provincial and National tournaments.

As Kelowna grew in population in the 1960s, the City responded by establishing a plan to grow sports facilities to keep pace. The first public face of that planning was the Parkinson Recreation Centre, opened in 1972. With a swimming pool, playing fields, tennis courts, and indoor gymnasium facilities, it demonstrated a true civic commitment to sports in Kelowna. Since then, other community facilities have come on stream.

As Rutland grew, a new centre was in order there. The Athens Pool was built in 1981, and over the ensuing decades the adjacent lands have seen the addition of ice rinks, playing fields, a gymnastic centre and the new home of Sport Kelowna. Organized for the first time in 2001, Sport Kelowna is charged with bringing the widest array of sports opportunities for Kelowna's citizens through sports development, sports tourism and sports partnerships.

In the 1990s, something new came along in the form of Public/Private Partnerships. This new approach to providing

With Kelowna's Chinatown as a backdrop, a rugby team is competing in Kelowna's City Park.

public services allowed the construction of huge new facilities while keeping the public tax burden to a minimum. The first of these in Kelowna was contracted with R. G. Properties for a new multipurpose sports and entertainment complex. Built in 1999, Prospera Place was the home of the 2004 Memorial Cup winners – the Kelowna Rockets Hockey Club. This first "PPP" was a success, and in 2004 the Capital News Centre opened in Okanagan Mission as part of a much larger and more comprehensive sports complex.

A unique tribute to those who have kept the sporting spark alive and well in Kelowna is the growing set of books and articles on the history of various sports in the City. R. Whillis, wrote a history of Lawn Bowling in Kelowna; Roy Kerr and Tip Harvey assembled and published *A History of the Kelowna Cricket Club*; Evelyn Metke worked assiduously to research and write a history of Golf in Kelowna; and Ursula Surtees collected a fine set of sporting photos, called *The*

Games Grandpa Played, for the City's 75th birthday and for the simultaneous hosting of the B. C. Summer Games. Together, these let us know how far we have come in one hundred years. They also assure us that sports in Kelowna have helped define who we are as a community of champions and great competitors.

If there were a pattern to the development of sports in Kelowna, it would recognize an increasingly keen level of organization, a move toward a more professional approach, and certainly it is more broadly based today. City facilities combine with individual drive, team investment and community spirit to insure the next one hundred years bring even more enjoyment and success.

The Kelowna Golf and Country Club's major water trap has always been an attractive feature for photographers. Here, probably in the 1930's, this scene was part of a series that featured significant amenities in the city.

Okanagan Oil

The 1930s scurry to discover oil in Kelowna generally focused on drilling in the Mission area. The first efforts, however, were actually in Capri's Five Bridges area in the spring of 1913; little came of those first explorations.

In November 1930, drilling began by the Okanagan Oil and Gas Co. Ltd on its Well No. 1. By the same time the following year their test hole had reached almost half a mile into the earth's surface and was hitting "...cretaceous marine limestone with every indication that the formation is the capping over the productive area."

It took the company another two years to get an additional 500 feet deeper and, while the company geologist claimed oil had been found, little financial support was forthcoming. By the fall of 1933 the company owed the Workman's Compensation Board almost $1000.00, and it seems this was paid by selling off redundant drilling equipment. With a need for approximately $10,000.00 to continue work, a November meeting of the company Directors suspended operations. What held hope for economic growth during the 1930s depression had proved an illusion.

Beginning about 1910, teams of shunting horses were used to shuttle rail cars on and off the barges that hauled them to Okanagan Landing and the C.P.R. mainline.

Riding the Rails to Kelowna

By Wayne Wilson

The Canadian Pacific Railway tracks joined Canada's Atlantic and Pacific coasts in the mid 1880s. Within a few years the Shuswap and Okanagan Railway built a spur line south from Sicamous, to Okanagan Landing. In her diary from 1891, Lady Aberdeen wrote of the rail trip south, *"A great part of the journey lay through very pretty country, extremely pretty after leaving Sicamous, skirting the edge of Mara Lake and then through some real big wood, and happily only a little of it burnt; then we came to Enderby half-way between Sicamous and Vernon where is quite a little town springing up on the Spallumsheen – as far as this a steamer can come, but from this point we were quite on a new track and we bumped and swerved along in a most marvellous fashion and at times had to creep along at foot's pace – it is indeed only just possible for a train to pass over and large gangs of men are working it still. As we came near Vernon we passed some very settled country and coming as we did, determined not to expect too much, we began to think that things looked very well."* (Lady Aberdeen, October 14, 1891)

This new rail link would be one of the keys to opening the region to further agricultural development. But the rail line was not immediately built further south to Kelowna. Instead, freight was shipped on sternwheelers to and from Kelowna and other points along Okanagan Lake. This transhipment worked well for a few years and it helped Kelowna keep pace with settler traffic, but Kelowna's citizens continued to feel left out of the railway boom.

A crew of more than 100 men worked to bring the C.N. rail line to Kelowna. Here, that crew lays the final few rails near Ellis Street on September 11, 1925.

Kelowna's rail connection to the outside world began in earnest, however, just before World War I. In about 1911, simple rail yards and a barge slip were built in the city's north end. From here, and for the next 14 years, freight traffic was shipped north to Okanagan Landing and from there on to the C.P.R. mainline at Sicamous. It might also have been shipped south to Penticton to be transhipped on the Kettle Valley Railway. During this time, thousands of railcars of Okanagan tree fruit products were sent around the world.

Kelowna's citizens certainly wanted a rail link to the outside world, but it was not to be. Land developers by the name of MacKenzie and Mann purchased acreage in the north end of town and reserved space for a station house; City Hall lobbied provincial and federal politicians to build the line to Kelowna; citizens' letters to the editor and other correspondence articulated the community's sentiments. World War I, however, brought an end to any real hope as efforts and money were put elsewhere.

The call for a rail link was taken up again quickly after the war, and this time there seemed some real value in investing in such construction. After all, the thousands of acres planted to new orchards just prior to World War I were coming into full

Opened in 1927, the C.N.R.'s Kelowna Station was a wonderful new addition to the community. The massive double-pitch roof gave the building presence, and the gardens facing Clement Avenue offered visitors a pleasant welcome.

bearing – and packing-houses need some form of smooth, cheap, and reliable transportation. A railway was the solution.

Until the mid 1920s, there were no locomotives in Kelowna. Instead, rail cars were moved along the various sidings connecting the packinghouses and warehouses with the rail yards and barge slips by shunting horses and later, shunting trucks. In 1925 the scene in the north end's rail yards changed forever with the driving of the last spike by Mayor Sutherland on Friday, September 11th.

That afternoon a crew of more than 100 men laid rail and drove spikes to complete the Canadian National Railway line to Kelowna. The newspsper noted, "In the midst of a very large gathering, Ellis Street was crossed at 2:30 and when the locomotive reached the station at 3 o'clock it blew its whistle and was answered by all the whistles of the various factories in the city."

Shortly after passenger service was established, the CNR brought in new sleeper cars for the Kelowna to Vancouver run. Named the "Kelowna" cars, they were, "Upholstered in attractive green fabric, the seats are luxurious for day travel and when the berths are made up at night coil spring mattresses – introduced for the first time to Canadian National Kelowna passengers – give promise of restful sleep."

For roughly forty years the CNR offered passenger as well as freight service. Much of that time, it seems, passenger service was a slow part of the business, and the company tried several ways to improve patronage but to no avail – probably a victim of increasingly efficient automobiles and ever more reliable road and highway networks. Freight traffic, on the other hand, remained strong.

Two marshalling yards formed part of the city's rail complex. The CPR rail yards ran inland from the lake just north of the Yacht Club. From there, its rail barge slip stretched into the lake. The CNR rail yards were further north and were hemmed in by Bay Avenue on the north and Clement Avenue on the south. A curious gateway to this area was the water tower that stood on Ellis Street across from the CNR station.

Passenger traffic continued to decline through the 1950s and ceased altogether in the early 1960s. Rail barge traffic remained in service for another 20 years when it too was cancelled, in 1979. Railway freight service continues today, but the volume and frequency of its distinctive sounds had diminished significantly. Residential and commercial development continues to squeeze north from the city's central business district on Bernard Avenue, and with that pressure, the railway will feel new realities. Whether its survives as a new commuter service or disappears altogether will depend on both planning and vision for Kelowna's future.

Sulky racing at the Kelowna Fairgrounds in 1918.

Kelowna and the Spanish Flu — 1918

By Sharron J. Simpson

When the Great War broke out in 1914, over 1,000 young men were mobilized from every Okanagan community and shipped off to become part of Britain's wartime army. Many were British settlers and remittance men who had settled in the Valley during the previous 20 years and felt compelled to return and defend their homeland.

The once-a-week edition of *The Kelowna Courier and Okanagan Orchardist* kept track of the medals, campaigns, and deaths of these young men, and by the fall of 1918 was reporting the imminent end to the fighting. However, local stories and fruit market reports took up most of the space in the newspaper and there was little mention of the influenza outbreak that had been devastating Europe and had recently arrived in Canada on the troop ships landing in Halifax. Neither was there any indication that the epidemic was making its way across the country on the transcontinental trains carrying battle-weary soldiers home.

Between October 9, 1918 and November 2, 1918, over 1,600 people died in Toronto. Over 2,500 people died in Saskatchewan during November, but still there was no hint of these catastrophic numbers in the Kelowna newspaper.

No influenza cases had been reported in the small town by October 23, although the dreaded disease had already made its appearance in Vernon and Oyama. Dr. W. J. Knox, the city's medical officer, advised Mayor D. W. Sutherland to prepare an isolation hospital in the old school (now the Brigadier Angle Armoury on Richter Street), and with the special emergency powers given to municipalities, the mayor also ordered the closure of all places of amusement, churches, schools, lodge meetings, and pool rooms as an additional precaution.

Dr. Knox, alarmed by rumours of imminent catastrophe, decided he needed more information and soon caught the sternwheeler out of Kelowna to Okanagan Landing, where he boarded the train to New York City. He was back home in less than two weeks, having learned that a virulent pneumonia accompanied the influenza and was the primary cause of the astounding number of deaths. Previously healthy individuals, many between 20 and 40 years of age, were dying within 12 hours of the onset of symptoms, and since penicillin would not be discovered for another 11 years, there was no treatment.

On his return, Dr. Knox found the community consumed by rumours of a 'flu outbreak in Chinatown – the area between Abbott and Water Streets and Harvey and Leon Avenues. On examination, he discovered there were four – and soon six – deaths, and the area was immediately quarantined. Only Chinamen wearing a white linen tag issued by the Chief Constable were allowed on the streets.

Knox warned others to isolate themselves immediately the flu symptoms appeared and take plenty of time to recuperate. As an additional precaution, all citizens were advised to cough and sneeze into a handkerchief and not spit on the floor or sidewalk.

A separate hospital was set up for the Chinese in a house on Ellis Street while another location was designated as the Japanese hospital. As more cases developed, Dr. Knox moved the community hospital to the high school (on the corner of Lawrence Avenue and Richter Street) and called for any citizen with a spare bed to deliver it to the emergency hospital. He also asked for any ladies who could step in on short notice to act as nurses and that donations of food, broth, and clothing be dropped off at the new location.

By November 19, the worst was thought to be over. According to the *Kelowna Courier and Okanagan Orchardist*, nine Chinese men died, along with one Hindu, and one Japanese, and while there were over 200 influenza cases in the district, these were the only deaths recorded. Kelowna seemed to avoid the worst of the dreaded epidemic.

In reality, it took two more years for the Spanish influenza pandemic to finally run its course and during those years, several prominent families lost both parents and children to the illness. But in 1918, as battle-scared young men returned from the European front and brought the dreaded Spanish flu with them, Kelowna's relative isolation – the train wouldn't arrive in town for another seven years – plus the efforts of a cautious medical officer – kept the impact of the epidemic to a minimum in the small community.

PHARMACY

In 1975, the Cameron family opened Black Mountain Pharmacy at 139 Highway 33 in Rutland. That tiny store was the beginning of a legacy that continues to grow. Over 30 years later, there are four I.D.A. Pharmacy locations in the Central Okanagan, all focused on preserving the excellent service and community pharmacy feeling of that one early store.

Black Mountain IDA Pharmacy now resides in the Willow Park Shopping Centre in Rutland, a move they made in 1980. Many expansions and renovations later, the store occupies about 6,200 square feet of the mall and includes a full service postal outlet and Sears outlet.

Glenpark IDA Pharmacy opened in the Glenmore area of town in 1996. Located in the Glenpark Village Mall, this 4,400 square foot pharmacy was the first to take residence in the fast growing Glenmore community. There is also a full service Postal Outlet in this store.

Mission Centre IDA Pharmacy resides in the new Mission Centre Building, which was constructed in 2003. Mission Centre IDA is a prescription centre, meaning that it has a smaller front store area than the other stores, but still maintains a full service pharmacy.

Lake Country IDA Pharmacy joined the family in 2004. This Winfield Pharmacy was recently expanded and renovated to better serve the Lake Country area.

A familiar site in all of these IDA locations is the Rexall brand of products. This popular and extensive line of merchandise recently celebrated it's own 100th birthday, and continues to offer premium products at affordable prices.

As this local company continues to expand, they have taken on new partners and become Paragon Pharmacies. Their head office is less than one block away from the original location of Black Mountain Pharmacy in Rutland, a reminder of where they started and what they want to do: integrate the latest technologies into their stores while continuing to provide community pharmacy with a focus on caring for customers.

Okanagan Lake Floating Bridge

When it opened in 1958 Kelowna's floating bridge was "... the first lifting span pontoon bridge in the world." Begun in January 1955, the bridge took two and a half years to complete. Twelve huge concrete pontoon sections measuring 200' X 50" wide and 15' high were built in dry docks at the foot of Cawston and Clement Avenues, then floated into place at the lake's narrowest point.

Held in place by a cable and anchor assembly attached to each pontoon section, there is ample flexibility to accommodate the rise and fall of the lake level throughout the year. The assembly also allows the bridge to move safely under constant wind pressure.

While a floating bridge was finally built, the original report called for a suspension bridge and, "On the basis of costs and aesthetics the design of a suspension span was started." Additional testing, however, revealed a poor geological substrate for building such a structure; "The foundation material was found to be very compressible under earthquake loading..." With that report in hand, engineers turned their attention to an equally challenging exercise – a 2100 foot floating bridge with an accompanying lift span. On July 19, 1958, H. R. H. Princess Margaret and Premier W. A. C. Bennett cut the ribbon to open the bridge and tie the Okanagan Valley together at Kelowna.

The 30th British Columbia Horse was the Okanagan's Militia, or Citizen/Soldier unit between the World Wars.
This unit comprised of a mix of wartime veterans of the 2nd Canadian Mounted Rifles and younger men.
Here, the Regiment is on maneuvers on the highlands south-west of Vernon, known as the Commonage. The
photo shows two of the three squadrons marching past 'in column of route'.

The British Columbia Dragoons

by Keith A. Boehmer

Between 1884 and 1908, the memory of the Riel Rebellion and the Alaska Border Dispute of 1903 encouraged the formation of various militia units in the Interior of British Columbia. One of these was the Okanagan Mounted Rifles, which was organized in 1908 in Vernon. By 1911 the unit had grown and became the 30th BC Horse (30thBCH) with squadrons in Lumby, Armstrong, and Kelowna, headquartered in Vernon.

In 1914 the core of the unit volunteered for active service in a new unit called the 2nd Canadian Mounted Rifles (2ndC-MRs). After several months in Victoria they were sent to England for further training, this time as infantry for trench warfare. From October 1915 to November 11, 1918, they served valiantly in every major battle Canadians fought in France and Flanders. For example, they filled the gap in the line during the June 1916 gas attack on the Canadian lines when forward units were decimated. They advanced across Vimy Ridge approximately where the Vimy Memorial stands today. In April 1919, they returned home to the Okanagan.

The old 30th BCH and the veterans of the 2nd CMRs formed a new Militia unit called the BC Mounted Rifles, later changed to BC Dragoons (BCD), in March 1920. Through the 20s and '30s the unit trained as cavalry. The Ministry of Militia purchased the old school on the corner of Richter St, and Lawrence Ave. as a 'temporary' amory in 1935. The unit is still using it today. Regimental Headquarters alternated between Vernon and Kelowna according to where the Commanding Officer lived at the time.

In 1939, Nazi Germany's 'Blitzkrieg' tactics put an end to any use of horse mounted cavalry units on the modern battlefield. Initially, the BCDs mobilized as a motorcycle unit patrolling Vancouver Island. Later they converted to tanks and went to England to train as the 9th Canadian Armoured Regiment (BCD). Meanwhile, the reserve unit recruited and trained in the Okanagan. The 9th CAR fought through the Hitler Line near Rome, and the Gothic Line in northern Italy. They then shifted to Holland for the closing months of the war. Kelowna orchardist and Militia cavalry officer, Harry H. Angle commanded the regiment in battle and brought it home in January 1946 to a victorious welcome.

During the early years of the 'Nuclear Age' the BCDs again reverted to reserve status and continued armoured training. Then a new trend flashed across the country to convert the Reserves into 'National Survival' units tasked with aid to civil power, and search and rescue work in the event of nuclear war. Unit morale and recruiting fell significantly until the 1960s when they converted to the light armoured reconnaissance (recce) role. This meant that if the Warsaw Pact forces invaded Western Germany, BCDs would join the Lord Strathcona's Horse (RC), western Canada's Regular Force armoured reconnaissance regiment, for battle in Northwest Europe.

1967 saw the awarding of the Guidon, or Colours, to the regiment by a member of the Royal Family. This is a silken flag with heavy gold and silver embroidery depicting the unit's badge and motto, surrounded by ten battle honours, on a scarlet with gold fringes. During the 1980s the BCDs changed back to armour with the allocation of four tank trainer vehicles called Cougars.

To mark Kelowna's 75th anniversary, the BCDs hosted the Okanagan Military Pageant. Several Okanagan communities awarded "Freedom of the City" proclamations to the unit during the '80s and '90s. Kelowna had bestowed this honour in June 1967. It is a tangible expression of civic pride and trust by allowing a unit "to enter and parade in the city with colours flying, drum's beating and weapons borne," without prior permission by civic authorities.

Various members of the unit have joined Regular troops in deployments overseas such as Cyprus, Germany, and the former Yugoslavia. Social visits to England, Holland and Italy renewed

City of Kelowna

KelownA
MEMORIAL
PARK CEMETERY
1991 Bernard Ave.
Kelowna, BC
862-5518

The City of Kelowna operates Kelowna Memorial Park Cemetery located at 1991 Bernard Ave. east of Spall Road. The cemetery occupies 50 aces of land adjacent to the Kelowna Golf and Country Club at the base of Dilworth Mountain. Originally an Anglican Church burial ground at the turn of the century, Kelowna Memorial Park Cemetery now pays silent tribute to the many different ethnic communities whose pioneer spirit built our city. Kelowna Memorial Park Cemetery has handled approximately 14,500 interments between 1894 and 2002.

This is the 'Colours' or 'Guidon' of the British Columbia Dragoons. The design follows old English Cavalry traditions and records the names of the battles which members had fought in during World Wars I and II. The Guidon is carried by the senior non-commissioned officer and escorted by two other NCO's, indicating the tradition of soldiers carrying and protecting the Colours in battle.

old ties and honoured the unit's fallen heroes. The Cougars were removed from service early in the new century and the unit faced tough proficiency tests to stay on the 'Order of Battle" as a recce unit. The regiment travels to Wainwright, Alberta for major training several times a year. In 2003 the unit was deployed as part of the extensive Canadian Forces contingent fighting the wild fires near Barriere and Kelowna, during Operation Peregrine. Today, the unit is expanding, with plans to reinstate the disbanded 'C' Squadron in Penticton. Regimental Headquarters and 'B' Squadron remain in Kelowna with 'A' Squadron in Vernon. 2008 will be their 100th anniversary.

The Raymer Block stood on the corner of Bernard Avenue and Water Street. With stores on the ground floor and an Opera House on the second floor, the downtown landmark was lost to fire in October 1916.

Fire Protection

By Wayne Wilson

By the time Kelowna was incorporated in 1905, the community had experienced enough trouble with fires that it needed to take action. In the summer of 1904 a horse drawn fire pump called the Broderick was purchased from Vernon and a year later a 250 Gallon Per Minute gasoline driven pump was purchased. Though neither piece of equipment was completely satisfactory, they did add substantially to the traditional 'bucket brigade' that typified pioneer communities.

Fire fighting stability really began in 1908 when the new city began to lay water mains and to put fire hydrants in the downtown area. By the beginning of World War I, Kelowna boasted an official Kelowna Volunteer Fire Brigade with custom-built fire trucks. This Brigade was housed in a Fire Hall built on the southwest corner of Water Street and Lawrence Avenue, purchased by the City in July 1906 and built by local contractor, M. J. Curts for a total of $785.00.

This first wooden fire hall served for almost 20 years until a new brick fire hall was built in the same location over the winter of 1924 – 25. As the town grew, the hall was added to and renovated numerous times from 1940 forward.

Within a few years of the City's incorporation, volunteer fire fighters were in place and training with equipment purchased by the City. Here, circa 1911, the crew poses for a photograph that was made into a postcard by one of the Valley's earliest photographers, G.H.E. Hudson.

88

FROM CANADA'S FIRST BANK
HAPPY 100th ANNIVERSARY KELOWNA

Bank of Montreal corner of Bernard & Water Streets in 1911

Photo courtesy Kelowna Museum

BMO Financial Group - founded in 1817 as Bank of Montreal, Canada's first bank - has evolved into a world-class, highly diversified financial services provider.

Bank of Montreal provided Canada's first sound and plentiful currency and has played a major and continuing role in the development of the country, taking part in the financing of the first transcontinental railway in 1867, and serving as Canada's central bank until 1935.

With more that 33,000 employees, BMO provides a broad range of commercial, retail, and wealth management solutions. BMO serves clients across Canada through BMO Bank of Montreal, BMO Harris Private Banking and BMO Nesbitt Burns, one of North America's leading full-service investment firms.

BMO Bank of Montreal has been part of the Kelowna scene since even before the incorporation of the City. In November 1904, an office was established on Bernard Avenue, on the site of the Bennett Hardware Store. The Bank proved to be a "boon to the growing community of Kelowna, where there had previously been many shortages of cash." The Bank was established at a time when it was transitioning from a cattle town to the centre of a major fruit growing industry.

An early branch manager, P. Dumouling, was instrumental in seeing that the community received ample support for the waterfront and for a cottage hospital, where he served as the first President. The greatest and most talked of project, however, was the construction of the beautiful bank manager's residence, known as "Hockelaga". Succeeding Bank of Montreal managers carried on the tradition of hosting hundreds of guests for an annual summer garden party and regatta at the Hockelaga mansion and grounds. Sadly, the building no longer exists.

Kelowna Main Office Branch has served the community continuously from the corner of Bernard Avenue and Water Street since 1908.

Our ongoing commitment was confirmed in 2002 when the Bank unveiled a new, 20,000 square foot, three-story building at the same corner, in the revitalized downtown core. Along with BMO Bank of Montreal's personal and commercial branching business, BMO Nesbitt Burns and BMO Harris Private Banking are also housed in this new, stately building. Under the leadership of Don Marr, Vice President, this location serves as headquarters for BC Central & Interior District. The 115 employees at our five Kelowna branches are excited about the anticipated population growth in this dynamic area of the Province.

As one of Canada's largest businesses and as a responsible company that believes in good corporate citizenship, BMO Financial Group also has a key role to play in helping to ensure that Canada's regions, towns and communities, like Kelowna, remain strong and vibrant.

BMO Financial Group is not only a witness to the progress that the City of Kelowna has made, these past 100 years, but also sees itself as a partner in that progress. As we enter our 101st year, the employees of Bank of Montreal extend best wishes to the citizens of Kelowna - may you continue to thrive and prosper for another 100 years!

In the years after World War II, Kelowna began to grow quickly – in terms of both population and its legal boundaries. In the 1960s Glenmore was added to the City's responsibilities and in the early 1970s the provincial government extended the civic boundaries to the south, east and north to make it one of the province's largest municipalities. The Kelowna Fire Department, as it became officially known in 1976, kept pace by purchasing new equipment, building new fire halls and adding more personnel with a wider range of skills. As the City turns 100 years old, Kelowna employs over 100 fire fighters working out of 7 Fire Halls, and responds to thousands of calls every year.

In March 1961, almost an entire city block was razed as flames leapt from one packinghouse to another. From this blaze, only the Laurel Packinghouse and its adjacent cold storage building were left standing.

A look back at Kelowna fire fighting history shows two eras of particular interest – times that gave the Department pause to reflect on its role in the community and gave the community a deeper appreciation of their work.

In the 1960s a series of devastating fires tore through one packinghouse after another. The most encompassing of these was perhaps the fire that levelled almost an entire city block between Ellis and Water Streets south of Cawston Avenue in 1961. Now the site of the Rotary Centre for the Arts, the Kelowna Art Gallery and the provincial Court House, this fire leapt from one building to the next despite the fire fighter's efforts. At one point, a locomotive was hooked up to parts of the buildings to pull them

Photo courtesy H. Brust

Kelowna's Heroes

apart and stop the spread of the fire. Though an arsonist was suspected, none was ever arrested. The experience, however, brought a new and keen focus on the needs of the community.

As Kelowna has grown outward, some of its residential areas have moved into lands on the fringe of the surrounding forests. In the summer of 2003, climatic conditions combined with a build up of forest debris to create conditions ideal for tragedy. A lightening strike in Okanagan Mountain Park in August ignited the forest floor and by the time the fire was under control it had spread east into Kelowna's city limits and destroyed more than 200 homes, thousands of acres of forest, and numerous other buildings.

The fire storm of 2003 brought the community together and it brought the Kelowna Fire Department an elevated place in the community. As the Department approaches its own Centennial, it will look back at 100 years of service that became increasingly sophisticated in its approach to fire and increasingly tied to the people it serves.

Celebrating our first century.

In 1906, Colbert Coldwell and Benjamin Banker began a real estate company dedicated to satisfying customers' needs. Today, Coldwell Banker has more than 3,600 offices and 114,000 sales professionals worldwide, including our award-winning affiliate **Coldwell Banker Horizon Realty**, right here in Kelowna.

Now, as Kelowna celebrates its centennial, Coldwell Banker is getting ready to celebrate an anniversary of its own. For nearly a century, we've been bringing people home. Founded by owners licensed in real estate in Kelowna since the mid 70s, Coldwell Banker Horizon Realty opened its doors in 1990 as the first Coldwell Banker franchise in Western Canada. As we helped make dreams of home ownership come true for our Kelowna neighbours, we earned a place for ourselves as a leader in the Coldwell Banker global network. Coldwell Banker Horizon Realty has earned the International Premier Office designation, being the #1 Coldwell Banker office worldwide for its office size in the number of homes sold and the International President's Award of Honour. We are the #1 Coldwell Banker company of its size in the nation in total production*.

So today, when you choose a Coldwell Banker Horizon Realty sales associate, you get the support of a knowledgeable professional, who knows this community and is backed by nearly a century of service and the most innovative resources in the business. We've come a long way since Mr. Coldwell and Mr. Banker started it all with one office and a simple dedication to service nearly a century ago. Happy Birthday Kelowna! We look forward to another century of serving home buyers and sellers in our beautiful community and around the world.

Coldwell Banker Horizon Realty
250-860-7500 * 1-888-KELOWNA
www.KelownaRealEstate.com

* Number One Canadian Office in both commission income and units sold in size category 36-50 sales representatives as of year-end 2002 and 2003.

The original root cellar and chapel still on the Father Pandosy Mission site.

Completing the Circle
THE DE PFYFFER'S AND FATHER PANDOSY'S MISSION

By Alice de Pfyffer Lundy

John Paul de Pfyffer was finding it increasingly difficult to support his large family on his lawyer's income in Lucerne, Switzerland, and by 1908 decided to explore the possibilities of immigrating to Canada. With his 16 year old son, Ralph, Paul sailed across the Atlantic and proceeded westward by train, stopping periodically to see if he liked the surroundings. It was a tiresome journey but when father and son stepped off the sternwheeler at the dock in Kelowna, Paul commented that "this looks like home." With that observation, Paul left Ralph with a local farmer, returned to Switzerland, sold his law practice, collected the rest of his family, and returned to settle in the Okanagan.

Joining Paul in this adventure into the wilderness were his wife, Hilda, sons Max, aged 20, Ludwig, 13, and Karl, 10, as well as daughters Eugenie, aged 15, Alice, 8, and Helene, 1. Albert, the 18 year old, remained in Switzerland to finish his course in civil engineering and joined the family when his studies were finished. Three maids and three dogs completed the entourage and after an unexpectedly long journey – no one anticipated the great distances that had to be covered – the family finally arrived in Kelowna, in the fall of that year.

The local newspaper of November 5, 1908 noted that "Doctor Paul Pfyffer von Altishofen had to run the gauntlet of real estate men from Sicamous to Vernon" upon the family's arrival – land sales were booming at the time. The same article went on to explain that Paul had decided to purchase the 15 acre Father Pandosy Mission site from the South Kelowna Land Company, who had earlier purchased the property from Father Pandosy's Oblate order. The site included three original buildings – the chapel, built in 1859, and the root house and Brother's house built in 1865 – the latter was

A family gathering with friends - Paul, Hilda, and Helen de Pfyffer are on the
left of the photo.

substantial and became the family's home. The paper also mentioned that "being devout Catholics, the Pfyffers will prove a welcome reinforcement to the ranks of other Roman Catholics in the district."

While the school-aged children attended the Mission Creek School at the corner of Benvoulin and KLO Roads, Paul became a "gentleman" farmer at what he called the Mission Ranch. About this time, Paul also changed his name, dropping the 'von Altishofen' and adding the 'de' in front of Pfyffer – the de Pfyffer name continues to this day. Paul grew tomatoes and onions and continued to operate the original orchard planted by the Oblate lay brothers in the 1880s. As was the custom in the early years, Paul always wore a suit – even when working in the fields – and soon became an active member of the Kelowna Growers Exchange. He also joined his neighbours in hiring Chinese labourers to harvest his crops.

Paul became fully involved in the life of the small community and left evidence of this in his many Letters to the Editor of *The Kelowna Courier and Okanagan Orchardist*. He was outspoken on a number of subjects

including the return the growers were receiving for the sale of their vegetables, and of his support for a central, single clearinghouse for the fruit and vegetable industry – which eventually became a reality though he was ahead of his time with the suggestion.

Eighteen years after their arrival, Paul received a small inheritance and since his wife was suffering from poor health at the time, he decided to take Hilda and their youngest daughter, Helen, back to Switzerland in the fall of 1927. By this time, the family farm had grown to thirty-four acres and Paul was comfortable leaving his prosperous investment in the capable hands of his sons. The couple never returned to Canada. Paul died in Lucerne in 1934, and Hilda died in 1946. Helen remained in Switzerland and Alice later returned, though both periodically visited their brothers in Canada and when some had moved on, in the U.S. Following the death of his parents, Max de Pfyffer, the eldest son who had remained in Kelowna, was appointed to dispose of the family's holdings.

By the early '50s the Father Pandosy buildings had become quite dilapidated and were slated for demolition. It wasn't long, however, until the community recognized their historic significance and with the intervention of Shorty Collett, Lawrence Guichon, Bishop Fergus O'Grady, of the Order of Mary Immaculate (OMI) and Father James Mulvihill, OMI, the decision was made to save the buildings and preserve the site.

The Oblates of Mary Immaculate purchased Father Pandosy's abandoned Mission, plus 20 acres of land, in 1954. In 1958, they added footings and new roofs to the original buildings before re-dedicating them as part of the celebration of the Oblates 100th anniversary of service in B.C.

In 1966, the Okanagan Historical Society and the Father Pandosy Knights of Columbus did additional work to restore and preserve the site, which by then, was owned by the Bishop of Nelson. In 1983, the site was officially designated a B.C. Heritage site.

In 1992, Bob de Pfyffer, grandson of Paul and Hilda, the Swiss settlers, in his capacity as Chair of the Okanagan Historical Society's Executive Council, signed a 50-year lease with the Bishop of Nelson to maintain the site in partnership with the Father Pandosy Knights of Columbus.

Twelve years later, in 2004, Alice de Pfyffer Lundy, Paul and Hilda's granddaughter, became the Chair of the Father Pandosy Mission Committee with a mandate to again revitalize and refurbish the Father Pandosy site. It has become a challenge for many organizations to preserve our province's heritage resources in an era

The Oblate Brothers house which became the de Pyffer family home in 1909. The house was later destroyed by fire.

of shrinking public funding, but Alice has a vested interest in maintaining the property: It was her grandparent's home and where her family's story in the New World began – it is part of her heritage and she is committed to its survival – not only because of her own connections to the site, but also because it is one of Kelowna's most popular and well-visited Kelowna heritage sites. The site is in good hands – circle is complete – at least for now.

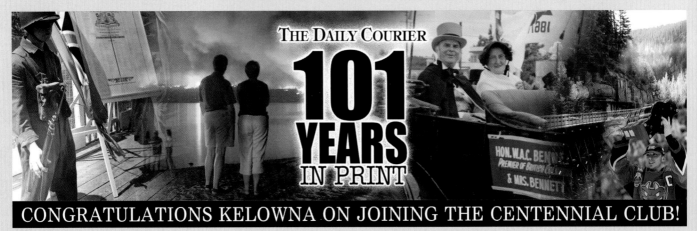

Centennial Month 100 years Ago

One hundred years ago newspaper reporting was a very different occupation from today, and the contents of the pages tell just how different. In the first case, most of the content came in over telegraph lines from other sources. In 1905, local news only represented about half of each issue.

Kelowna's first newspaper was called the Kelowna Clarion and Okanagan Advocate, and it started publishing on July 28, 1904. The following year it was sold and the new owner, George Rose, changed the name to the Kelowna Courier and Okanagan Orchardist. Published weekly, the May 1905 issues shows an emerging city that was busy with comings and goings of its citizens, with the concerns of the new municipal government, with new business interests, and with just plain fun.

Thursday, May 4, 1905
Dr. Boyce opened a new office in the former Post Office, and perhaps its most noted feature was its fine new paint job. The Knights of Pythias held their parade the previous Sunday and the reporter assured readers that it was not to have been missed.
An editorial drew citizens' attention to the growing problems of irrigation, and it was hoped that the brand new City Council could find ways of equitably dividing the precious resource.
Both W. C. Cameron of Guisachan and G. R. Thomson of Creigilea in Okanagan Mission had potatoes for sale. The latter had 18 tons of them!
An advertisement enticed readers: "Why drink heating whisky these warm days when you can get the cooling cider at Bankhead Ranch."

Thursday, May 11, 1905
The cover of this issue held Kelowna's Proclamation as a new City in the province of British Columbia.
Polo season was under way at Guisachan with 14 members of the Kelowna Club in attendance.
Planning was well under way for Victoria Day celebrations that would see the community treated to boat and pony races and all other manner of sports.

Thursday, May 18, 1905
The Canadian Pacific Railway announced there would be weekly refrigerated rail service to the Valley.
Dan Gallagher set out 150 trees in his Mission Creek farm site and the planting was thought to be the first in that area.

Thursday, May 25, 1905
There were so many trout in Mill Creek and its adjacent irrigation ditches that people reported catching 8 to 12 inch trout by hand!
A new large addition to the Lakeview Hotel on Abbot Street was announced.
G. F. Budden and J. J. Stubbs had been hired to repaint St. Michael and All Angels Church and had the job well under way.

The Kelowna Daily Courier still brings the community the news, and it was joined between 1908 and the early 1920s by the Orchard City Record and in 1930 by the Capital News.

preserving *the* past... creating *the* future

2004
CULTURAL CAPITALE
CAPITAL CULTURELI

MEMORIAL ARENA

reflect

The cultural district is a rich architectural landscape with many of the landmark buildings protected by heritage status. Discover the transformation of retired fruit warehouses or tobacco plants into intimate galleries or nightclubs.

celebrate

Help us honour the past and celebrate the future by joining us May 5, 2005, for Kelowna's 100th birthday celebration and the 2nd Annual Life & Arts Festival May 6-8.

Kelowna's Cultural Distric
British Columbia • Canada

For more information on
Kelowna's Cultural District, or
to book a guided tour contact us at
1-866-903-3384, or visit
www.KelownasCulturalDistrict.con

Arts and Culture

Pioneer settings are often seen as bustling centres of business life whose only purpose is to transform the new landscape into a setting that is 'modern' and is 'organized: road networks are laid out, settlement is divided into business, industrial and residential districts, and, eventually, a local government helps provide some forward planning for that growth.

But life is not all about work - and Kelowna's pioneers were quick to incorporate arts and culture into their activities, Local groups performed plays and light operas, still others organized literary events. All of this was supported by talented and often formally trained resident artists, dancers, writers and musicians.

In particular, over the last half of Kelowna's first century, that talent has come together in a more formal way and the municipality has gotten behind its citizens efforts. Construction of the Kelowna Community Theatre gave a locus of theatrical activity; construction of the Museum in 1967 strengthened heritage appreciation; establishment of the Kelowna Art Gallery in the 1970's helped stabilize the visual arts; and construction of the Rotary Centre for the Arts more recently has given Kelowna's Cultural District a critical mass. And that critical mass will bring delight, awe, thoughtful reflections and artistic inspiration for generations to come.

One of Kelowna's first artistic expressions, the Kelowna City Band, has been entertaining citizens for almost 100 years.

Probably taken at the Kelowna Opera House about World War I, this photo shows how intimately tied to the arts and culture groups the business community was at the time. It is a tradition that continues today.

ROTARY CENTRE FOR THE ARTS
Kelowna's Cultural Venue

A home for arts, music, education and entertainment in the Okanagan. Located in the heart of Kelown'a Cultural District, the Centre houses the 332- seat Mary Irwin Theatre, eight resident artists, a bistro, box office, pottery studio, a board room, galleries, dance studio, rehersal hall, greenroom and set shop.

For events, course information, room rentals, please contact (250) 717-5304 or visit: www.RotaryCentreForTheArts.com

...there's nothing like seeing it LIVE!

Wait until Dark 1977

Checkerboard Guy 2002

Dads:The Musical 2000

For the Pleasure of Seeing her Again 2001

Since 1962, we have been home to Kelowna's vibrant performing arts community and a popular touring venue for regional, national and international performing artists.

You can win free tickets for upcoming events just by visiting our website at KelownaCommunityTheatre.com. You can also get event information by calling our phone marquee at 469-8940.

KELOWNA COMMUNITY THEATRE

Chinatown

British Columbia's pioneer communities were most often a collection of cultural groups from the east and the west. Kelowna was no different in this regard.

Kelowna's Chinatown occupied 2 to 3 city blocks in the Lawrence/Leon/Harvey Avenue and Abbott/Water Street area. Home largely to single men who had often worked on the railway or in the province's mining industry, the community grew to a population of about 600 at its largest.

As these men grew older and passed away, the properties in Chinatown were sold and torn down to make way for new development. For those who had families here, Kelowna's Chinatown remains a legacy of their cultural connection to the pioneer experience.

Chinatown's early pioneers.

David Lloyd-Jones on the left with friend Sam Miller in
Mr. Lloyd-Jones' 1907 Tudhope McIntyre

One of the Earliest Pioneers

DAVID LLOYD-JONES

By Sharron J. Simpson

When David Lloyd-Jones died on June 13, 1944, a brief article appeared in *The Kelowna Courier* noting the event, explaining that wartime "paper restrictions do not permit an outline of his activities at this time, but a sketch of his life will appear in next week's issue." It never did.

However, the following week City Council did observe a moment's silence as an expression of their high esteem for the "grand old man whose good citizenship and unpublished kindness was recognized in the community and throughout the Valley." Lloyd-Jones was also the last surviving member of the 1905 City Council – the first after the city's incorporation.

David was born in Burford, in the Lake Simcoe region of Ontario, where the lure of the west seemed to capture the imaginations of many young men in the area. His brother, William, convinced David to join him in British Columbia where they planned to preempt land and become cattle ranchers – no experience was apparently necessary. By the time David took the Union Pacific Railway across the U.S. to San Francisco (the CPR was still five years away from becoming

Canada's transcontinental railway) and caught a steamer up the West Coast to Esquimalt (near Victoria), William had moved on and was working as a carpenter at the Postill Lake Ranch, near Winfield.

With instructions from his brother on how to reach the Okanagan, David caught a small boat across Georgia Straight to New Westminster, then the booming metropolis of the Lower Mainland, and transferred to a steamer to travel up the Fraser River to Chilliwack and on to Hope, where he was to join Eli Lequime's pack train and continue on to meet his brother.

However, the trip from Esquimalt to Hope had taken David three weeks and Lequime had given up waiting and departed three days earlier. At the age of 18, with his total possessions being a tool chest and $2.00 in his pocket, David found himself alone in the midst of the towering mountains with few resources other than his sense of adventure. As so often seems to be the case in pioneer tales, a couple of good samaritans crossed his path.

The first was Frank Richter (after whom Kelowna's Richter Street is named), another steamer passenger, who invited the young David to join him for the next part of the journey. The second was the storekeeper at Hope who, by this time, was pretty good at sizing up young men needing a grubstake. When David informed him of his meagre finances, the storekeeper apparently responded: " That's all right young feller, you'll make lots of money where you're going and I'll be paid in due time."

The small party headed off on horseback toward Princeton expecting to catch up with Lequime, but their delays had been long and the guide and his pack train were nowhere in sight. Richter was heading further south so when the pair arrived in Princeton, he pointed the trail toward Penticton out to David – likely not giving a second thought to the inexperienced young man who was about to head off into the wilderness alone. Richter's instructions were to find Tom Ellis, the well-known Penticton cattle rancher, who would put him up for the night and give him directions to Okanagan Mission.

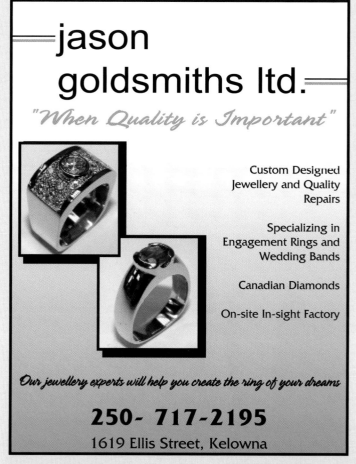

David rode on for hours expecting to see the green valley of the Mission each time he crested a hill, but each time he was confronted by another mountain. Being unfamiliar with wilderness travel, he had made no provisions for food and when he encountered a pack train heading south and they told he was only half way to his destination, he almost collapsed on the spot. As night fell, Lloyd-Jones finally rode into the Okanagan but when he encountered a fence which seemed to have no end, he was so exhausted he simply slid off his horse and slept where he landed. The next morning, the ragged pair finally met up with the elusive Lequime and after recuperating for a few hours, David finally made his way to the Postal Lake Ranch and his brother.

The two were experienced carpenters and when Lord and Lady Aberdeen built their new home at Guisachan, David was hired to work on the house, which remains as one of Kelowna's major restaurant and heritage sites. Soon after the Aberdeen's house was completed, the two brothers headed to Summerland where the commonage had been opened

for staking. The brothers took up land in the area eventually named after them - Jones Flat – and were able to finally realize their original dream of preempting land and become cattle ranchers.

By 1893, the Lloyd-Jones brothers decided to go their separate ways when William returned east and David headed to Kelowna to begin his long career in the sawmill business.

The Lequime family had decided to branch out from their Okanagan Mission base and opened a general store at the foot of what is now Bernard Ave. (named after Bernard Lequime). David's returned from Summerland was timely as he immediately set about building their store, and since they had worked together on this project, the Lequimes hired him to manage their saw mill and planing operation which just was across the street from the store.

The small mill employed about 15 men for six to seven months a year and had a capacity of about 15,000 to 20,000 board feet a day. David bought an interest in the

mill three years later, and by 1902 decided to purchase the balance of Lequime's holdings and become the sole owner of the small but productive Kelowna Saw Mill.

Fires are a fact of life in the sawmill industry and before David began working at the mill, the small operation had been almost burned out in 1896, and then again in 1899. When David took over in 1902, his first concern was that his new investment was adequately insured – but as he was making the arrangements, his sawmill burned to the ground. As he surveyed the ruins, a couple of the town's business-men offered him cash to start up again. A few years later, David made his benefactors his business partners and F.A. Taylor, T.W. Stirling and Arthur Day continued to reap the benefits of his successful opera-tion, until the business was sold in 1942.

Another fire destroyed the mill in 1906 but this time David had adequate insurance and was able to rebuild with little difficulty. However, each fire provided an opportunity for the Kelowna City Council to try to convince Lloyd-Jones to move his sawmill further north, away from the burgeoning business district along Bernard Avenue and the increasingly busy City Park. Rumor is that David would agree to the move – provided he was given 10 years forgiveness on his

municipal taxes – there is no evidence the City fathers ever accepted his offer.

By 1942, David decided it was time to sell his sawmill – by then he was 80 years old – though it apparently wasn't his intention to sell to his competitor, S. M. Simpson Ltd. However, when an offer came from Vancouver, David assumed the purchaser was from the Coast and agreed to sell. In fact, the bid had been made by an agent for Stan Simpson, who was primarily interested in the dilapidated mill's logging assets. It was wartime, however, and the area had box quotas it had to meet, so Stan kept the old mill operating until October, 1944, when another raging blaze finally destroyed the Kelowna Saw Mill.

Though the operation was insured, Stan Simpson consolidated its production with his newer operation at Manhattan Beach, and the site was subsequently sold to the City of Kelowna to become its Civic Centre. The Kelowna Saw Mill Company continued until 1957 as the retail arm of S.M. Simpson Ltd.

Always a gentleman, David Lloyd-Jones was known for his fair dealing and willingness to help anyone down on their luck. He is quoted as saying: "I have always tried to give any man the benefit of the doubt, and have tried to do right by the other fellow."

His name still resonates in the city today. The David Lloyd-Jones Home for Seniors on Bernard Avenue was originally the site of his family home, and the last and most modern of the ferries that crossed Okanagan Lake between Kelowna and the Westside, before the floating bridge was opened in 1958, was the *M.V. Lloyd-Jones*.

David's journey to the Okanagan was typical of the way many Interior settlers arrived in the Valley, and his adaptability in moving from one job to another – depending on the opportunity and the need at the time – also enabled him to flourish in this new land. Many followed in his footsteps but a few early Okanagan settlers stand out as successful adventurers . . . and David Lloyd-Jones was one of them.

The Kelowna Aquatic Fire

When City Park's Ogopogo Stadium and Aquatic Centre burned to the ground on Saturday, June 14, 1969, the community lost not only the home of its famous Kelowna International Regatta, but also its summer gathering place.

The blaze was reported in the wooden grandstand and within minutes the flames had engulfed the structure and quickly moved onto destroy the restaurant, the hall used for dances and community dinners, as well as the ground floor change rooms and boat storage sheds.

One report estimated that 5,000 people gathered to watch the blaze which had apparently been started by children playing with matches. The intense heat blistered paint on nearby signs and parked cars quickly became too hot to touch as onlookers tried to push them away from fire.

Fortunately, there was no loss of life and while the Regatta continued, there was much debate in the community about the wisdom of rebuilding the structure. In the end, the insurance money was added to other city funds and the Parkinson Recreation Centre – with its indoor pool – was built to replace the open stadium. Old timers still discuss whether this was the right decision, but the new facility provided the growing town with a new recreation centre which continues to be well-used to this day.

At the foot of Bernard Avenue, the CPR built a warehouse in 1906. The S.S. *Aberdeen* is in dock here and the array of freight on the wharf indicates something of the nature and volume of traffic.

Getting to Kelowna by Boat

By Wayne Wilson

Tucked into the folds of the Cordillera mountain ranges, pioneer Kelowna was like many new little communities – difficult to get to. Trails, many built along well known aboriginal routes, gave the first access to the Okanagan Valley. As population grew, these trails were improved by colonial administrations and later by provincial agencies and departments. It was not until the pioneers started to use Okanagan Lake as a major transportation corridor, however, that the settlement process was eased and speeded up.

Regular and reliable water transportation to Kelowna and other points along Okanagan Lake probably began in earnest with Captain Thomas Dolman Shorts in the early 1880s. With his 2.5 ton capacity rowboat, named the *Ruth Shorts* after his mother, he averaged about nine days for the voyage between Vernon and Penticton with stops in the Kelowna area along the way. His second venture, the *Mary Victoria Greenhow,* was launched on April 21, 1886, and its steam engine brought both speed and some limited reliability to his enterprise.

As settlers continued to find their way to the Kelowna area and a flotilla of little private vessels brought in their supplies, the Canadian Pacific Railway (CPR) was beginning to take notice. The volume of settlers encouraged the survey and naming of the City of Kelowna, which was laid out in 1892 by Bernard Lequime. At the same time, the CPR began construction of the first of its three great sternwheelers on Okanagan Lake.

The S. S. *Aberdeen* was launched at Okanagan Landing on May 3, 1893. She was 146 feet long with a beam of 29 feet. With 554 gross tonnage, she was capable of ample freight capacity and she had passenger staterooms too. For the first time, Kelowna residents could expect freight and passenger service as the S. S. *Aberdeen* called in at 1: 00 PM on the way south (Mondays, Wednesdays, and Fridays) and at 3: 00 PM on the way north on alternate days.

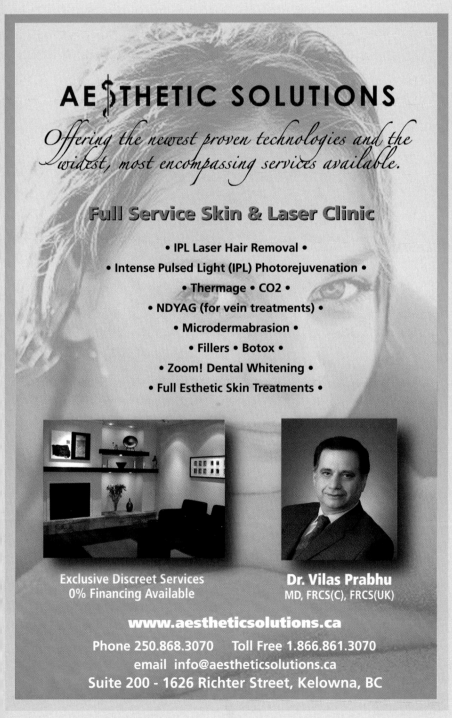

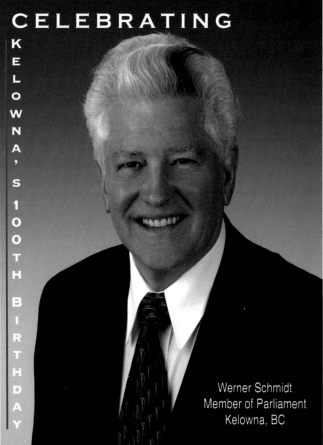
For the first few years, traffic was relatively light, but as prairie markets began to grow and as a succession of federal governments encouraged immigration, the sternwheeler traffic became steadier. Although the new century's land boom affected the entire Okanagan Valley, Kelowna entrepreneurs seemed to be particularly eager, as they purchased cattle ranches and surveyed them into 5 to 40 acre orchard lots. Between 1904 and 1914, thousands of acres were brought into production.

At the peak of this land boom, the CPR launched its second sternwheeler, the S. S. *Okanagan*, on April 16 , 1907. With a gross tonnage of 1077 tons, she was 193 feet long and 32 feet wide. The two ships kept pace with settlement in Kelowna, docking at the wharves at the foot or Bernard Avenue. Sometimes they even hauled barges to keep up with freight demands.

Such business must have buoyed the CPR's hopes, because on May 19, 1914 they launched the Valley's most famous and elegant sternwheeler – the S. S. *Sicamous*. At almost double the gross tonnage of the S. S. *Okanagan*, she was also able to carry more than 300 passengers as well as freight. With silver cutlery, linen tablecloths, a 65 foot dining room, staterooms, and excellent food and service, the ship spoke well for new investors in Kelowna and the region. Decks and berths filled with passenger, their holds filled with cargo, and their secured areas filled with mail and other correspondence, these ships were Kelowna's vital link to the outside world.

For roughly twenty years the S. S. *Sicamous* served the region but, as the automobile and rail service improved, her days were numbered. In early January 1935, she was tied up at Okanagan Landing and declared out of service. For another 16 years she languished at the docks when she was bought by the City of Penticton and towed to its shores where she rests today.

In many ways, her replacement was a trio of ferries that crossed the lake from downtown Kelowna to the Westside. The *Aricia* perhaps provided the most consistent ferry service until the provincial government took over in 1927 with a 15 car capacity ship. The first of the steel hulled vessels, the M. V. *Pandozy,* was launched in 1939. Within a few years the M. V. *Lloyd-Jones* was added; and in July 1950 a third ferry, the M. V. *Lequime*, was launched.

Although Kelowna boasted a rail line from 1925 forward, rail barge traffic remained an imprtant transportation option until 1979.

The post World War II economic boom saw Kelowna and the region grow substantially – in population and in economic diversity. The most significant internal barrier to continued development was the ferry link at Kelowna. In 1958 that final barrier was removed, with the opening of the floating bridge, and the trio of ferries was pulled from service.

Supporting this transportation complex over the years was a cadre of tugboats, barges, company boats, and private vessels. For almost 70 years a rail barge service plied the lake, and tugs still move some log booms to the sawmill at Manhattan Point. Together, these boats and ships gave Kelowna an air of economic stability that drew continuing investment and that gives its history an archive full of wonderful stories and compelling images. Commercial scale shipping from Kelowna's wharves is now a legacy of pioneer effort and vision.

The M.V. *Pendozi* was one of three car ferries to help join the north and south parts
of the Okanagan Valley at Kelowna. The trip across the
lake took only a few minutes.

This is a postcard photo taken by early Kelowna photographer, G.H.E. Hudson of the Curtiss biplane that entertained crowds on the beach in Kelowna in August 1914.

Flying in to Kelowna

By Wayne Wilson

In the Archival files of the Kelowna Museum is a folder filled with newspaper clippings and typewritten notes on the history of aviation in Kelowna. From shortly after 1900 to today, it is a story of increasing connections to the outside world.

Beginning in 1914 at one of the City's early Regatta events, Kelowna pioneers saw, perhaps, the Valley's first airplane. A Curtiss biplane took off from the City Park beach to the wonder of all and photographic postcards were shot to commemorate the event.

More regular air service to the city began in 1927 when an airstrip on the upper benches of Rutland was put in to commission. From here, Radium Hot Springs Air Services provided both instruction and what was probably the region's first charter service.

Through the 1930s and until after World War II, the Rutland field proved an adequate strip for Kelowna's and the Okanagan's needs. New post-war demand for service, however, saw the city looking for a new site that could be expanded. In 1946, the City purchased land in the Ellison District and immediately built a 300 foot wide by 3,000 foot long airstrip. The strip was completed in 1947 and the same year a small terminal was added to the site. The following year the airport was licensed.

Over the next ten years the airstrip became more heavily used by both private pilots and commercial operations. In 1957, the Federal Department of Transport worked with the City of Kelowna to construct a new gravel runway, and

The Elsie was operated by Dominion Airways, and this photo of one of their floatplanes
was taken on the beach in City park, probably in the 1930s.

within two years, a paved runway was begun. In the summer of 1960, a new 5,350 foot paved runway hosted regular Kelowna-Vancouver flights by Canadian Pacific Airlines.

The 1960s was a watershed decade for development at the Kelowna International Airport – a new runway, new terminal building, new safety equipment were among the upgrades. The decade closed with the scheduling of regular jet aircraft service between Kelowna, Vancouver and Calgary by Canadian Pacific Airlines.

Since then the airport has expanded steadily to accommodate ever increasing passenger service, to incorporate technological improvements, and to position the facility as the Interior's premier international airport. To accommodate increasing commercial traffic, the airport parking apron was expanded in the early 1970s, and a decade later a new helipad was added.

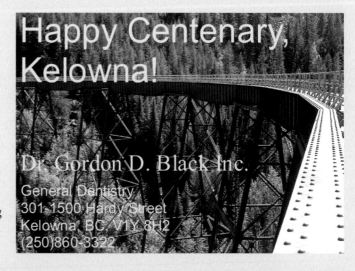

Once at the orchard, water was distributed to the trees along a series of ditches that ran down each side of the trees.

The Greening of Kelowna

IRRIGATION - CATALYST FOR CHANGE

By Wayne Wilson

Between 1904 and 1914, much of the Kelowna area began to change from brown to green. The catalyst for that change was irrigation. Long, elaborate, and expensive systems of water storage and distribution were built to criss-cross the bottomlands around the city centre and across the benchlands that overlook it.

The water came from the upland lakes that flank the main Okanagan Valley trench. Postill Lake, Beaver Lake, Belgo Lake, and many others were dammed just prior to World War I. The increased water storage gave early orchardists something they desperately needed – a ready and reliable supply of water for irrigation during the hot summer months.

These dams were the first part of the system, but they certainly were not the most visible. For orchardists and early investors in Kelowna, the intricate network of canals, flumes, and siphons told a more impressive tale of economic investment and success.

Canals and ditches, carved into the soils or blasted out of the rocks, wound their way along the hillsides and overlooked the orchards below. Where these structures could not be built, impressive flumes carried water over gullies and canyons.

Perhaps most curious piece of engineering in this system was the use of siphons to take water either over hills or across valleys. As long as the outlet was at a lower elevation than the intake, the system could draw and move huge volumes of water long distances with ease and safety.

Once at the orchard, the water was distributed to the trees along a series of narrow ditches that ran down each side of the rows of trees. These "furrows" needed to be monitored constantly to avoid washouts, but the result of this careful water management made the area's agricultural land shine bright with the green of thousands of acres of symmetrically manicured trees – truly, the "Greening of Kelowna."